I0889731

PENGUIN BOOKS

SELF-IMPROVED ME

Puty Puar, an Indonesian and a mother of two, was born in 1989. She works freelance as an illustrator, content creator, and book author. She integrates her blog and social media across platforms to deliver heartwarming and relatable visual content that aligns with her purpose of empowering women from within and her belief in the collective power of women to create massive and long-lasting impacts. She also shares her experiences through sharing sessions, talk shows, and workshops.

She is the founder and executive director of Buibu Baca Buku, a community aiming to empower women, especially mothers through literacy and reading habits.

In 2018, Puty won the JCS International Young Creative Award, a part of the International Emmy Award 2018. In 2023, she received the Good Chat, a fellowship for Southeast Asia community leaders and influencers aiming to mainstream the climate conversation. It has led her to learn about sustainable development these days.

Find her at byputy.com or Instagram @byputy

Self-Improved Me

An Illustrated Guide to SELF-DISCOVERY and Continuous Improvement

PUTY PUAR

PENGUIN BOOKS
An imprint of Penguin Random House

PENGUIN BOOKS

Penguin Books is an imprint of the Penguin Random House group of companies
whose addresses can be found at global.penguinrandomhouse.com

Published by Penguin Random House SEA Pte Ltd
40 Penjuru Lane, #03-12, Block 2
Singapore 609216

Penguin Random House SEA

First published in Penguin Books by Penguin Random House SEA 2024

Copyright © Puty Puar 2024

All rights reserved

10 9 8 7 6 5 4 3 2 1

The views and opinions expressed in this book are the author's own and the facts are as reported by her which have been verified to the extent possible, and the publishers are not in any way liable for the same.

Please note that no part of this book may be used or reproduced in any manner for the purpose of training artificial intelligence technologies or systems.

ISBN 9789815266153

Typeset in Poppins by MAP Systems, Bengaluru, India

This book is sold subject to the condition that it shall not, by way of trade or otherwise, be lent, resold, hired out, or otherwise circulated without the publisher's prior consent in any form of binding or cover other than that in which it is published and without a similar condition including this condition being imposed on the subsequent purchaser.

www.penguin.sg

For Isa, Nala, and Anggun

CONTENTS

INTRODUCTION

Being a woman in this modern society is getting more challenging each day. There are a lot of expectations from our closest ones and even pressure from strangers on the internet.

'When will you get married?'

'When will you have children?'

'Why does your child behave that way? You must be too busy working.'

'Do you even like your job?'

'You haven't joined any Pilates class yet? Like, ever??'

'Beyoncé also has twenty-four hours in a day, you know???'

They seep into our minds without realizing it, creating guilt and making it difficult to be aware of ourselves and what we truly aim for. There are times we do something only out of fear of missing out because everybody seems to be doing it (or at least, that's what social media tells us). Should we just stop using social media altogether, so we can stop comparing ourselves to people we don't know on the internet?

Unfortunately, as social creatures, human beings naturally compare themselves with others. *Self-awareness and mindfulness about our purpose are the first steps to gaining clarity in life.* They are part of the self-discovery journey, where we honour our growth process and embrace our imperfections.

This illustrated book offers a sort of toolkit that breaks away from a one-size-fits-all method. It's about the process of discovery itself.

good grades! but when will you get a job? hurry up and start hustling!
good job, but when will you get married? hurry up and start finding the right partner!
good wedding, but when will you have children? hurry up before you get too old!
good! but don't you invest too little time on him? aren't you too busy with your career?

With bite-sized writings and illustrations, it aims to help us get to know ourselves better and appreciate our unique way of progressing in life. It includes exercise templates and practical tips for arranging our priorities, measuring our progress, and making better decisions based on self-reflection and evaluation.

The Unending Battle : Comparison

CHAPTER 1

THE UNENDING BATTLE: COMPARISON

Why We Compare Ourselves to Strangers on the Internet

Have you ever felt tired of feeling miserable after checking LinkedIn or scrolling through your Instagram timeline? Have you wondered if you're a bad, greedy, or envious person because you don't have that designer bag all your friends seem to have? (Where did they get the money from?)

If there's one takeaway from this book I'd like to share upfront, it is that *you will always compare yourself to others*, no matter how many motivational quotes on Instagram or Pinterest tell you otherwise. There are scientific explanations for this: We are social creatures, and our brains always measure where we are compared to others for evolutionary reasons. This process is subconscious and happens naturally. Comparing ourselves to others is a way to identify our social status, and social status has been a cue to ascertain who has control over what resources since premodern times. It is hardwired in our brain to understand our position compared to the others because higher status brings more food, more territory, and better health care. In short, higher status means a higher capacity for survival and reproduction, so our brain keeps trying to do something about it (Storr, 2022).

ANCHORING EFFECT

So, the next time you can't help but compare your 'A Day in My Life' video with some mid-tier social media influencer's, do not feel bad. It's normal to be insecure about not having that overpriced tumbler, you know, the one the rest of your yoga gang have. If you try to ask yourself, deep inside, the answer might be that you just want to be accepted or feel superior among your peers.

Or, to quote Céline from the movie *Before Sunrise* (1995), 'Isn't everything we do in life a way to be loved a little more?'

Another proof of comparison being innate is a behavioural phenomenon called the anchoring effect. The anchoring effect is a cognitive bias that causes us to rely heavily on the first piece of information we are given about a topic (Tversky and Kahneman, 1974). When making plans or estimates about something, we interpret newer information from the reference point of our anchor instead of seeing it objectively. This can skew our judgement and prevent us from updating our plans or predictions as much as we should.

For example, if you want a bag that was originally $1000 but is on sale next week for only $300, you will consider it a good deal. This bag might be more appealing than another one priced initially at $250.

The problem with comparison is that our 'relatively ancient' brain hasn't evolved to deal with so many references. While our ancestors compared their power with their tribe members or maybe the guys from the other tribes, we now deal with endless anchors that make our boats too heavy and, sometimes, stuck.

Understanding the science behind our need to compare ourselves to others will hopefully stop us from doing what is impossible and start mitigating this issue more strategically.

We compare ourselves to strangers on the internet, but what's next? How can we navigate it so that the insecurities that kick in don't affect our journey?

Self-Improved Me Note

- Accept the fact that we naturally compare ourselves to others.
- Navigate the feelings that come so they will not be distractions in our journey.

Words Have Context, Pictures Have a Thousand (Unspoken) Words

We compare ourselves to strangers on the internet—that's one thing. We also compare ourselves to people we know in real life, which is another problem. Sometimes, this is even harder to navigate.

When my mom was in her twenties, she resigned from her job at a hotel and became totally happy with her life as a homemaker, raising two kids and keeping the house comfortable. I couldn't relate to this. When I quit my job and started to work from home, I felt restless, even though I made that decision myself because I wanted to take care of my family.

The difference between me and my mom was probably that she didn't have to deal with social media. I checked LinkedIn and saw a lot of female colleagues doing well in their careers, and I couldn't help but feel left behind. I was still connected to my friends on social media and found out that those who once were struggling with me at university were travelling the world while I was stuck at home, dealing with uncertainties (and awful clients!) as a freelancer.

On the other hand, my mother was only in touch with some friends whom she had been talking to from time to time, so when she heard good news like business success, she also understood what that friend had been through. She had enough backstory to contextualize someone's success. When she saw the life of a superstar on TV, she hardly felt envious because the context was clear: that person was a celebrity.

life Reference

Nowadays, in this hyperconnected era, we see many references and hypothetical possibilities with very little context. Those who are not married think they would be happier if they were just like that friend on Instagram who recently shared a photo from her child's first birthday bash. Those with stable 9–5 jobs think their lives would be easier and more flexible if they quit and run their own businesses.

We have such little time to dig into the backstories of every success because everything is so fast-paced. We are often trapped in the narrative of: 'If that person can do it, why can't I?' Not that being competitive is bad, but if we make everything a competition, we might win some battles but will lose the whole war.

Self-Improved Me Note

When you feel bad about yourself when you read or listen to successes or happy stories, take your time to think about these questions:

- What precondition might exist behind the success? What kind of unspoken words might be there?
- Does someone's happiness negate your own? (Hint: It should not.)

The Paradox of Plenty: Too Many Options Can Steal Your Joy

All the seemingly good social media posts and the narrative of 'If that person can do it, why can't I?' give us the illusion that we have unlimited choices and could have done things differently. You might feel regret from hypothetical decisions you think you could have made. I once came across a joke by someone on an Instagram reel saying that she regretted not starting *that* YouTube channel ten years ago because if she had, she would not have to go to her 9-5 job at a bank the next day.

Curve of Happiness vs the number of choices *

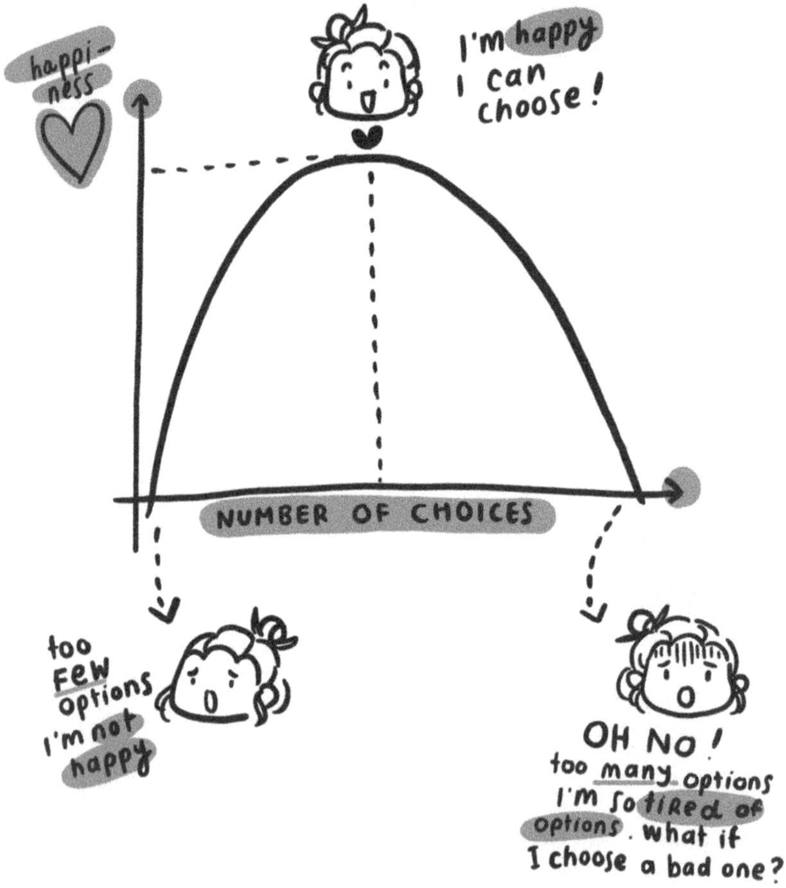

(Curve adapted from Elon Musk's interview on Business Insider, 2020)

This sentiment is not unfounded. It aligns with a study by Dan Gilbert where he conducted an experiment on people to choose one of five free art prints by Monet. Without knowing the experiment, the participants were divided into two groups; the first group could exchange their art print of choice, while the second group couldn't change their minds. After a few weeks, the study revealed that people in the second group were more content about their choices (Gilbert, 2007).

Similar things happen in the dating scene these days. In his book, *Modern Romance*, Aziz Ansari mentioned that it might be harder to find 'the one' on dating apps because we're given this illusion that we may find someone better. It lets us wonder, 'What if my truest soulmate is a couple of swipes away?' It didn't happen to people from older generations. They had a smaller dating pool, and the options weren't infinite (or seemed so). When they met someone, they had fewer what-ifs than we do today.

In short, more options may lead to more happiness and better decisions, but only to a point; after that, they have opposing effects. *By recognizing this illusion of endless possibilities, of paths not taken, we can gain a clearer perspective on the different lives people lead and perhaps feel more empowered in our own choices.* Focus on living the life we have decided to, with all the ups and downs, without the unnecessary regrets and what-ifs.

Then vs Now: Modern Aspirations and Traditional Expectations

In general, Southeast Asia places a strong emphasis on family and social connections. The idea of women continuing the family legacy by becoming mothers holds varying degrees of importance across the region.

an Empowered girl back then...

a questioned woman now...

While there is a growing social acceptance of women pursuing careers and personal goals, societal norms still expect them to be the main person taking care of the family needs.

Many of us find ourselves in a unique position, born and raised during this transition. Our parents encouraged us to pursue the best education, believing that we, as women, could achieve anything. Yet, society still clings to traditional expectations, dictating that women should marry before thirty and devote themselves to raising children.

In Indonesia, many mothers resign from their jobs to care for their children. It is mentioned in the book *Beyond the Tiger Mom: East-West Parenting for the Global Age* that it is not uncommon for a mother to take a year off work to supervise her children's education, even in the highly urbanized and modern Singapore. These mothers are seen as responsible parents willing to do their best to help their children get the best education. Exam periods can be stressful not only for students but also for their families, especially the mothers (Thiagarajan, 2018).

These unrealistic expectations may lead to the feeling of not having enough or giving enough. Some of us might have experienced getting questioned about life choices by our older relatives during family gatherings, 'Okay, you're pursuing a doctoral degree, but what about your love life?' or 'You're a high achieving career woman, but what about your children?' In some cases, Independent women settle for less just so they can get married, while some mothers feel like they need to be more productive as stay-at-home-moms.

Let this serve as a reminder that we often find ourselves caught between our modern aspirations and the traditional expectations placed upon us. It's normal to feel overwhelmed, especially when support is lacking. But remember, there's no need to feel guilty. Take care of yourself, and don't hesitate to seek help when you need it.

Self-Improved Me Note

Receiving personal questions regarding life choices from our older relatives can be problematic. Keep healthy boundaries while considering their perspectives and recognizing the generation gap. You can tell them that while you appreciate their concern, you'd prefer to discuss certain topics only when you're comfortable. Otherwise, you can redirect the conversation and focus more on positive interactions. Talk about shared memories or things you have in common.

From News at Noon to Non-Stop Notifications: Keeping Up with Infinity

Another reason that people feel like they don't have enough or give enough these days is the rapid and fast-paced flow of information. There are new trends every day and breaking news every hour.

When I grew up in the early nineties, media was still very limited. We only watched cartoons once a week, and the news was only aired twice a day, one hour each session. People talked about more or less the same topics and gossiped about the same celebrities.

Thirty years later, today, it just seems impossible to be bored. New movies are released every week on different streaming platforms. Anyone can tell their stories, publish their music album, or create a webinar. While the creative scene is flourishing, we may get overstimulated. Furthermore, we became prone to the famous fear of missing out (FOMO). It's increasingly difficult to get by each day without feeling left out. On the other hand, our desire to conform and be accepted is ingrained in our brains. As human beings, we want to do our best to catch up to be in sync with others.

Catching up with the new trends and information these days:

Our unmatched desire to catch up can be an additional mental burden. It gets us to do what is not essential for us. Instead of spending time doing what we have to or want to do, we keep scrolling through our smartphones, get even more tired, and still feel like we do not know enough.

Let's take a moment to reflect. How often have you spent time watching a movie you weren't even interested in in the first place just because everybody else did? Have you ever queued at an overhyped restaurant just because it went viral on TikTok? *At what cost?*

Self-Improved Me Note

When you realize that you're about to do something out of FOMO, pause a bit and ask yourself these questions: What's the worst thing that may happen if you don't do it? What was the worst thing that ever happened to you when you missed out? Is it that bad?

When you feel like you are
NOT enough

CHAPTER 2

WHEN YOU FEEL LIKE YOU ARE NOT ENOUGH

Don't Compare Pears and Apples

We can't just shut ourselves off from the outside world to avoid exhaustion from distractions. Instead, the impulse to compare ourselves to others, succumb to unrealistic expectations, and do things out of FOMO should be overcome by trying to know ourselves better and being mindful of what really matters to us.

Imagine yourself in a sports field full of people on a peaceful afternoon. Everyone has come for different reasons. Some athletes prepare to practise for a sprint competition, and some elders are there for an afternoon walk and to clear their minds. A group of aunties is there hoping to lose weight, while some other aunties only want to move their bodies. Once you notice, you realize how different everyone's pace is. The good news is that you don't have to follow anyone. You can go for a brisk walk. You can also just stay still and watch them all while enjoying the late afternoon breeze. It is not a matter of winning or losing. All you need is to know why you decided to show up and what matters to you, and as long as you accomplish this, you win.

to compare fairly,
you need to compare
apples to apples.

but first and foremost
you need to fully understand
'what is an apple?'

Now if you want to compare
yourself to others, have you
fully understood yourself?
are you an apple? or are
you a pear?

In the bigger picture of life and timescale, we often forget who we are and why we're doing the things we're doing in the first place. When we forget, we get lost. We run when the athletes run just because we think we're one of them.

There's a phrase when comparing things, 'apples to apples', where it's only fair to compare similar things. However, to be fair, we must know what an apple is. We need to identify the characteristics of an apple and why it is categorized as an apple so we don't compare it to a pear.

Now, when it comes to ourselves, do we know ourselves enough to identify that we're apples and not pears?

Exercise Template

Uncovering Your Inner Compass

Who are you? What makes you different from others? What makes you 'you'?

Biologically, our DNA, the blueprint for our bodies, determines our physical characteristics and shapes particular traits and personalities that have something to do with our behaviours. Moreover, what makes us 'us' are our life experiences, closely related to our decisions and influenced by our values.

Back when I worked in a multinational company, I was lucky enough to meet many people who were wonderful in their own way. I had a high-achiever boss who reached an important position at a relatively young age because they worked so hard. On the other hand, I had a team leader who was very wise but not really someone you'd call ambitious. He worked hard but didn't hesitate to say no to work that conflicted with his family schedule. I, myself, wasn't married then and dreamed of reaching at least the vice-president level in a company. One day, I had a conversation with my team leader, and

WHAT IS IMPORTANT FOR YOU?

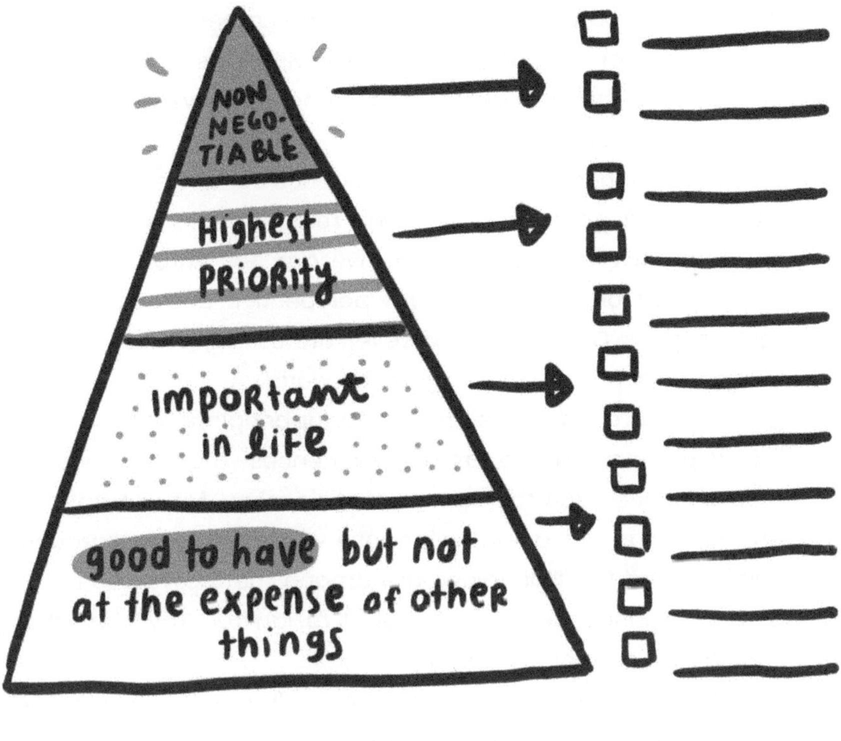

(Adapted FROM: 'The Design Thinking Life playbook' by Michael Lewrick et al, 2020)

I remember he said that his definition of success focused on his family's happiness. He was happy when he could have lunch with his son, even on work days.

It sounds simple, but it changed my perspective on defining success. Some people aren't really concerned about being at the top of the work hierarchy as long as they can be present for their family. Some people want a shining career and to make a more significant impact, while others wish for stability. Neither one is better than the other because people have different life values and priorities.

As mentioned before, values influence our decisions. Values influence our goals, priorities, and relationships—who we are comfortable with and with who we are not. Throughout life, there might be changes in our perspective and what really matters to us. Core values, however, are usually the foundation that determine how we navigate the world.

Values are usually related to our upbringing; how we were raised plays a big role, as do experiences—the things we go through in life—and the culture of our society. For example, as an Indonesian with a relatively conservative family background, religious and familial values are among the top values in my pyramid. It influenced my decision to resign from my job so that I could take care of my family.

There is likely to be more than one value you believe in, and some things might be more important than others. The order might also change along the way, but please look at the table, check the illustration of the pyramid of values in this chapter, and think about it.

What are your 'non-negotiables'? What are the priorities that follow your non-negotiables? What is good to have but not at the expense of other things?

Recognition
Autonomy
Movement
Honesty
Relaxation
Freedom
Leadership
Feelings
Belief
Idealism
Creativity
Love
Meditation
Courage
Order
Travel
Self-realization
Solidarity
Spontaneity
Environment
Knowledge
Work
Prominence
Relationship
Property
Development
Fairness
Joy
Care
Equality
Humour
Sensuality
Art
Loyalty
Compassion
Thinking
Partnership
Romance
Self-esteem
Excitement
Sports
Independence
Aesthetics
Career
Belonging
Personal responsibility
Success
Family
Friendship
Holistic nature
Justice
Harmony
Children
Standard of living
Pleasure
Curiosity
Politics
Tranquillity
Safety
Saving
Status
Trust
Affluence
Appearance
Progress
Honour
Influence
Nutrition
Figure
Peace
Feeling of security
Health
Intuition
Activity
Performance
Power
Music
Openness
Wealth
Self-sufficiency
Quest for meaning
Spirituality
Dream
Truth

Taken from *The Design Thinking Life Playbook* by Michael Lewrick, Jean-Paul Thommen, and Larry Leifer (2020).

These values also act as boundaries. It's not always easy to decide how much is too much and what line we should allow ourselves to cross. Will we take a job in the fast-fashion industry that offers an excellent salary? Should we accept an international assignment that requires us to do a long-distance marriage? *Being mindful of our values makes saying no to certain things easier. Being mindful of our values helps us to define what success is.*

And, of course, being mindful of our values helps us make healthy comparisons, apples to apples.

What Offends You the Most, Tells a Lot About You

Values can be the line where we draw boundaries. While they can keep us being 'us', they can also be a label we attach to our identity: family man, hardworking employee, kind boss, or even social justice warrior. Once something, consciously or not, becomes part of our identity, it is often the hardest thing to unlearn. In short, it's an area we need to be aware of when change is necessary.

For example, when you see 'friendship' and 'kindness' as higher priorities, you have the tendency to be 'the nice guy' or 'the kind boss'. If you have an underperforming subordinate with a bad attitude, it may be harder for you to confront him because, well, 'Aren't you that kind boss?' and confrontation is not something that others expect from you. You may also feel like it contradicts your identity.

In their book *Difficult Conversations*, authors Douglas Stone, Bruce Patton, and Sheila Heen point out that the most challenging conversations often have something to do with identity. *What offends us a lot, indeed, reveals a lot about us.*

What offends you a lot, tells a lot about you

Now, take some time to reflect on these:

- Acknowledge what really matters to you and what you might embed as a part of your 'identity'. Maybe you value independence a lot so it is hard for you to ask for help, or you always see yourself as someone fashionable so it hits you hard when someone questions your OOTD.
- How you can adopt the mindset that identity is not binary, it's not 'all-or-nothing'? It's not you're either good or evil, hardworking or lazy, devotedly religious or sinful. Think of identity as a spectrum. Be aware that you can be kind and fun while being strict with others professionally when necessary. Allow some room for you to grow in that spectrum.

Let values be the line where we draw boundaries, but not ones that stop us from growing.

MBTI: Most Behaviours and Traits Are . . . Incoherent

According to Carol Dweck, a growth mindset means believing that a person's abilities aren't innate but can be improved through effort, learning, and persistence (Dweck, 2017). A growth mindset is about the attitude with which a person faces challenges, processes failures, and adapts and evolves. Those who believe in and overrate someone's talent usually find it harder to adopt this mindset.

Relying too much on talent isn't the only thing discouraging us from having a growth mindset. *Believing that our personality traits are fixed and unchangeable also makes us think that some static factors determine our behaviour.*

come on, as someone who was born under LEO sign, you are supposed to be a natural party goer and attention lover!
whut?
NO, I'm an INFJ!
and I'm OLD.

For example, we might think, 'Virgos are perfectionists', or 'ENFPs have too many interests and little discipline', attributing our micromanaging tendencies or inconsistencies solely to our zodiac signs or MBTI quiz results. On the other hand, it's natural that we want to understand ourselves better. That's why personality quizzes are attractive, especially when they give a sort of validation to our past actions.

Aside from how these categorizations do not represent a suitable framework for understanding personality (Stein and Swan, 2019), this belief may also prevent us from learning and changing. For example, if you feel seen by your ENFP personality quiz result, you may subconsciously attribute it to the failure of starting your own business: 'Oh, maybe I just get bored too easily.' This will distract you from evaluating the situation objectively and identifying the real problem. Was it you or your marketing strategy?

As humans, we tend to be biased about the importance we attribute to personality. A famous experiment known as the Good Samaritan Study (Darley and Batson, 1973) investigated why people help (or don't help) others in need. The study was conducted in a seminary, with an assumption that students there were generous and religious. The seminary students were told to prepare a talk on the Good Samaritan parable, a story about someone helping a stranger. Without knowing, some students were given limited time so they needed to hurry, while others had plenty of time. On their way to the talk, all the students came across an actor pretending to be hurt and needing help.

Which seminary students stopped to help the hurt person? Those in a rush were much less likely to stop and help. This study revealed that a situation influences decision-making more than someone's core values and personality.

In short, stop thinking that your identity is inborn and static. You can change through time and adapt to different situations. You will evolve.

Self-Improved Me Note

- It's natural to feel validated by personality quizzes or zodiac signs but be aware that they don't define you and should not determine your behaviour. You can adapt, and you can change through time.
- Remember that situations influence our decisions more than our personality.

Self-Discovery: A Never-Ending Journey

The realization that our identity is ever-evolving opens the door to embracing new experiences and challenges which in turn allows for growth.

I have a friend who thought she wasn't good with people because she is an introvert. In high school, she hated parties and felt it was very hard to fit in. Years later, after she became a mother, she joined a family-education community as a member. As time passed, she felt comfortable with the community and got more involved as a facilitator. At first, she hesitated to take on more responsibilities because she clung so tightly to her perception of herself: She wasn't good at dealing with people.

However, with the right people and a supportive community, she discovered that she enjoyed talking to people with the same interests and purposes. Beyond that, she could contribute to a bigger team and become a leader. From that point, she learned a lot more about community and leadership. She realized she could be a good leader because she is purpose-driven, a good listener, and tends to maintain harmony in an environment.

self-reflection
self-awareness
self-discovery
self-improvement

She just discovered this and finally figured out why she wasn't comfortable at parties during high school—finding the right people to be with brings out the best in her.

I believe there are many similar experiences. Sometimes, there are new things we learn about ourselves after meeting the right people: friends, teachers, leaders, partners. *Self-discovery is a never-ending process that we are only aware of after we push, improve, and reflect on ourselves.*

Self-Improved Me Note

Think about these**:** Do you have any beliefs about yourself that are hard to unlearn? For instance, you believe that you're not good at dancing or you can't cook. Think about the circumstances that made you believe this at first and compare it to your situation today. Do you think it can change?

WHEN YOU feel like
YOU ARE not
Doing enough

CHAPTER 3

WHEN YOU FEEL LIKE YOU ARE NOT DOING ENOUGH

Blooming Like No Others, Just Like Others

Most flowers are not noticed until they bloom, yet we all bloom in different ways and at different times. When we think that life is a running competition, we might feel left out or far behind others. However, once we start to see it as a garden, it's easier to trust our process and keep going.

We bloom slowly, then all at once.

Not all 'Bests' Look Good

X, the academic, just shared that they presented their paper at an international conference.

Y, the activist, just shared that their non-profit initiative received an impact award.

Z, the illustrator, just shared that they collaborated with a big apparel brand.

We keep getting updates from people who are thriving and succeeding at doing their best. On one of 'those days', it might make us feel worse about how our own lives are progressing.

We just bloom differently.

sometimes doing your best looks like this . . .

but it may look like this too

On one of 'those days,' reading a motivational quote about 'trusting the process' might even make you want to punch someone in the face. (No offense taken.)

Let this be a little reminder that 'doing my best' might look different from one person to another. Even for the same person, it might look different from one day to another. Some days, it is about achieving the sales target or winning a competition, but on the unluckier ones, it might be just getting by (with sweat and tears).

Let this be a little reminder that self-improvement is not just about getting better or achieving more. It's also about getting tougher and being brave enough to try again, even if it feels like you're regressing instead of progressing. Sometimes, it's about starting again from zero after a devastating process of letting go.

It's not easy because it requires us to shift our perspective and zoom out. For example, breaking up with a boyfriend after a three-year relationship while your friends are getting engaged might feel like a gut-wrenching punch to your next five-year timeline plan. However, if you take another moment to see it from another point of view and zoom out to your twenty-year plan, marrying a toxic man will cost you much more in the long term, even forever. *So yes, it's a win. It's you doing your best.*

Self-Improved Me Note

How do we practice this perspective shift? Try to create a gratitude journal and fill it consistently. Write down one or two things you're grateful for and try to explore different kinds of gratitude. It might be about what happened and didn't happen, what you have and don't, whom you met and didn't, etc.

Today's Mantra:

I can't do everything
but I can do SOMETHING.
and for that something,
I'll do my best.
and my best doesn't
require any validation
from people on the
internet.

Exercise Template

Reverse Bucket List!

Have you ever heard of a bucket list? It's a popular concept—a list of experiences you wish to have before you 'kick the bucket'. It's a great way to dream big, push your boundaries, and create a life filled with adventure.

Now, let's make a reversed one instead. *A reverse bucket list is a list of things you have already accomplished.* Let's take a mindful pause and think about them. It's time to pat yourself on the back for the mountains you've climbed, both literal and metaphorical. Be proud of yourself and be grateful for those opportunities!

my reverse bucket list
got my writing published ☺
visited Japan
volunteering in a community
tried to build business from home
watched my fav band's concert

My Reverse Bucket list

- ✓ got
- ✓ tried
- ✓ visited
- ✓ watched
- ✓ visited
- ✓ touched
- ✓ bought
- ✓ met

PS: make as many pages as you wish!

Get, set, goals

life
can only be
understood
backwards,
but it must be
lived
forwards
(Søren
Kierkegaard)

CHAPTER 4

GET, SET, GOALS!

Beyond the To-Do List: Aligning Goals with Values

I once read a blog post about a girl who faced financial difficulties during childhood. She then promised herself that she'd do her best to pursue a decent education to secure a good job and bring joy to her family. Slowly but surely, she achieved her target, earning scholarships and getting a job in a consulting company, marking the milestones until her financial situation improved. At one point, her dream came true, and she was able to support her family. However, she got busier than ever. She didn't pay much attention to her father when he got sick and could only regret it when he passed away. This hit hard, but since then, she decided to allocate more time to care for her mother, her first and foremost reason for hustling hard in the first place.

You may have encountered similar stories or even experienced them yourself. We work so hard because we want to be able to afford good food, but then we get so busy we skip meals often. We work so hard so we can build a house with a swimming pool but when it comes true, we don't even have time to swim.

before setting the path FORWARD

take a step back to remind yourself of what REALLY Matters

Being mindful of our purpose and setting goals are essential steps in living forward. Yet, we often get too busy to revisit them as we get lost inside the to-do lists and calendar appointments.

I'm not telling you to quit your job here (really, in this economy?) What I'm saying is to take some time to check if you put what really matters on your priority list.

If you think that being family-oriented is among the top priority in your life, what kind of goals have you set related to this? Do you think it's time to put spending undistracted quality time with them at least once a week on your list? If you realize that health is critical, have you set a goal of consistently moving your body at least twice a week on the list? Or do your goals only cover your career and financial situation?

Self-Improved Me Note

Try to write down and reflect on your core values. Are your goals right now aligned with what's truly important to you? (Check your pyramid of values with the exercise template 'Uncovering Your Inner Compass'.)

Do You Really Want What You Think You Want?

Aligning our goals and values is trickier these days. The internet offers almost any answers, even for the questions you never asked in the first place. 'How to be rich', 'How to gain many followers in one night', 'How to raise a genius student', 'How to take the best picture in front of Mount Fuji, Japan', and so on. Most of the time, these answers are shoved down our throats endlessly on social media. People offer tips, tutorials, solutions, and sometimes 'cheat codes'.

What we don't realize is that we spend less time asking 'why'. We don't even question whether we really want what we think we want.

Let me tell you HOW to gain millions of Followers and BE a millionaire!!!
YOU WANT IT, RIGHT?
everybody wants it...
YOU DO! Follow me; I have the ANSWER.
HOW TO BE FAMOUS
wait, did I ever ask how to gain Followers? do I even want them?

'Why do I want to gain many followers?'

'Do I even want my child to be a genius at school?'

While setting your goals, besides reflecting on your values, try to add the 'why' question in addition to the 'what', 'how', or 'how much'. There is a thinking routine called the Three Whys that dives a little deeper into your head (Zook, 2018). You begin by asking 'Why is that?' to a statement, and then writing your answer down. After that, ask 'Why is that?' about your answer. Once you've responded, ask another 'Why is that?' about the second answer. Note that the last answer should connect to fundamental human needs and survival, such as safety, security, belonging, and self-preservation.

For example,

Statement: I want to have one million followers on social media.

1. 'Why is that?' Because I want to be able to influence people and make an impact
2. 'Why is that?' Because if I'm able to influence people, I can be famous and highly paid
3. 'Why is that?' Because if I'm famous and highly paid, I'll have power and privilege

This exercise helps you better understand your desires, whether they translate to the right goals and action plan, and how they can align with your values.

The internet knows all the how-tos, but only you know the whys.

Defining Productivity Productively

'I'm sorry, I'm fully booked this weekday.'

'Let's go have lunch together. Hmm, let me check. How about three weeks from now, from 11.00 a.m. to 1.00 p.m.? Let me send you the calendar invitation.'

In this fast-paced world, we often see busyness as a currency. We associate being busy with productivity, being well-connected, and being needed by others. We push or get pushed (or both!) to work more and faster. It's not strange that sometimes we feel we are not enough because we are not doing enough or achieving enough.

However, please be reminded that productivity is about how we can manage our resources to get the optimum results. The less resources spent, the better.

The expected results vary greatly depending on the context. For instance, a hectare of land can be considered productive in different ways. If it's a farm field, then it will be productive when planted with rice and producing crops. If it's a piece of land in the city, then the same area, or even less, will be productive when rented out and generating income. Understanding this flexibility in the definition of productivity can help us adapt our approach to different situations.

Do not feel bad about managing your time and energy your own way. Do not feel bad when you feel like your calendar is not that colourful or you are more available than the rest of your team members. Sometimes, less is more. Remember, some meetings could be an email. You can create a strategy to get your team to prepare their ideas before a brainstorming session. You can send your meeting material and rundown in advance to make a meeting more effective.

Productivity may look like
500 pages of a novel manuscript
but may also look like
5 pages of an academic journal

Self-Improved Me Note

TL; DR: Productive ≠ busy

Exercise Template

Wheel of Life—Start with the Present

'So where do I start with goal setting? How should I formulate my goals and action plan that align with my values?'

We can start with a tool called the Wheel of Life. The Wheel of Life was first created in the 1960s by Paul J. Meyer as a life coaching tool, which was later developed and adapted to life-coaching programmes (Una Byrne, 2005). The spokes cover eight aspects/dimensions of our lives, which generally include:

- Physical health
- Mental and spiritual well-being
- Relationships (family and friends)
- Physical environment (home and surroundings)
- Financial situation
- Business and career
- Personal development
- Fun and recreation

The essence of the Wheel of Life lies in reflecting on the quality of each aspect of our current life. To do this, we use a rating system from one to ten. Remember, every wheel is personal, so it's best to use your situation as a benchmark. For instance, if you feel financially secure today, rate it accordingly (eight or even nine!), without feeling the need to compare yourself to a millionaire.

The next step is to mark the score of each aspect and connect them all to see the shape of your Wheel of Life. Imagine this as the wheel that will take you along your life journey.

HOW ARE YOU, Really?

ASSESS with the wheel of life

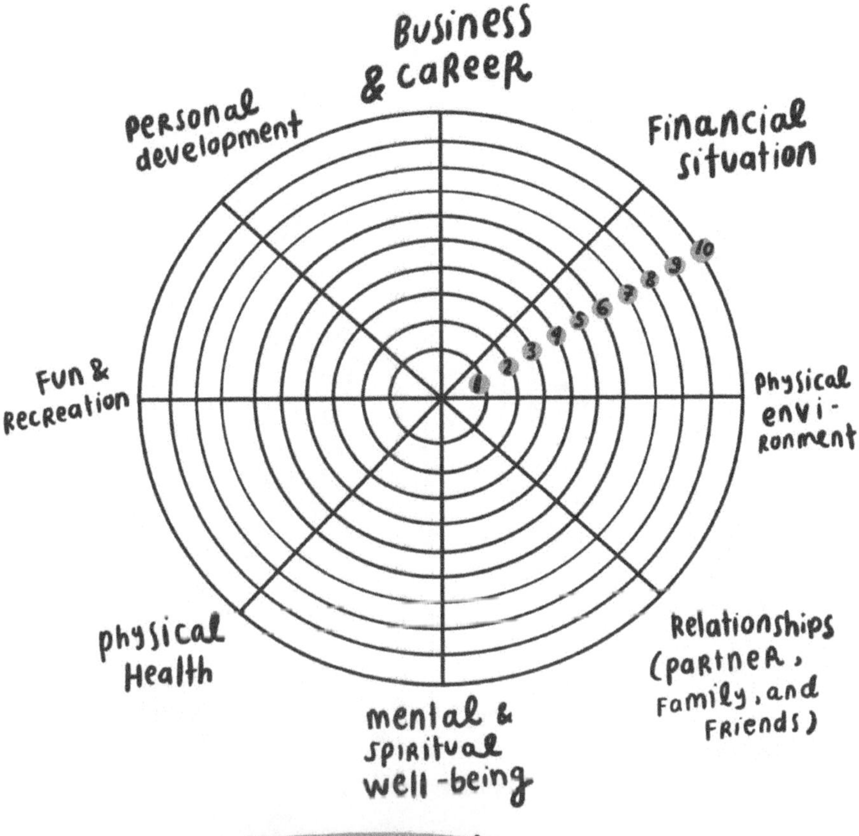

this is the original template. you may copy it on a blank paper! Find out how to use it on the next pages!

HOW ARE YOU, really?

ASSESS with the wheel of life

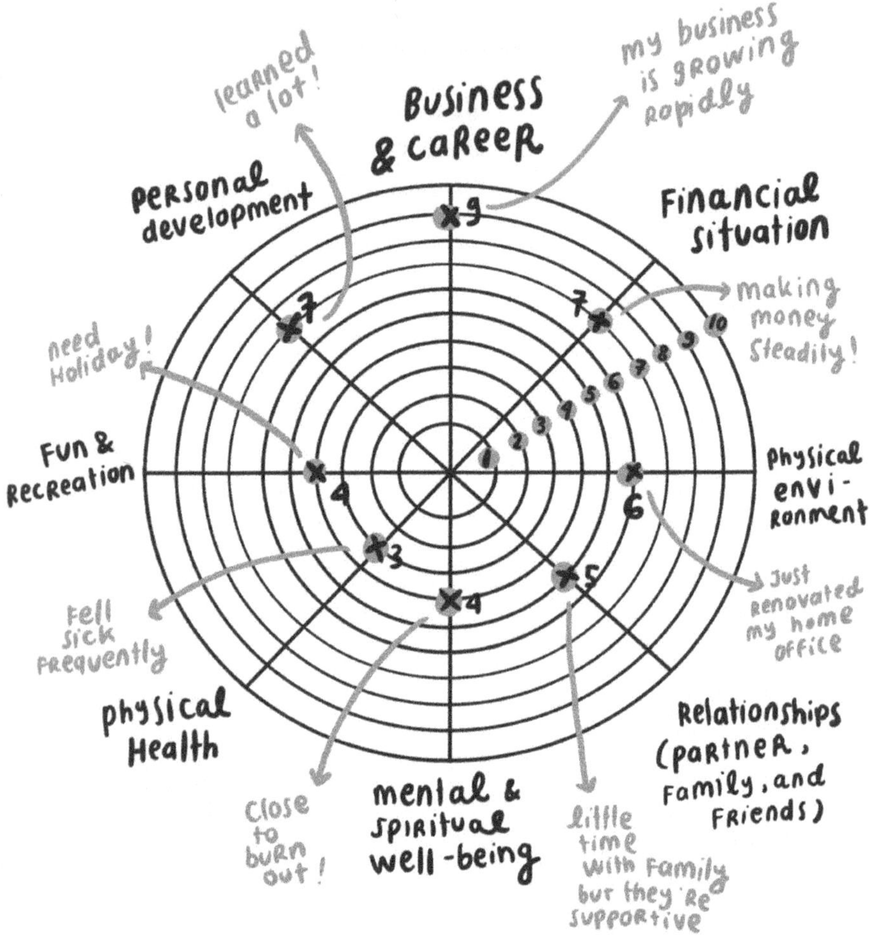

give scores to the different aspects of your life right now

HOW ARE YOU, Really?

ASSESS with the wheel of life

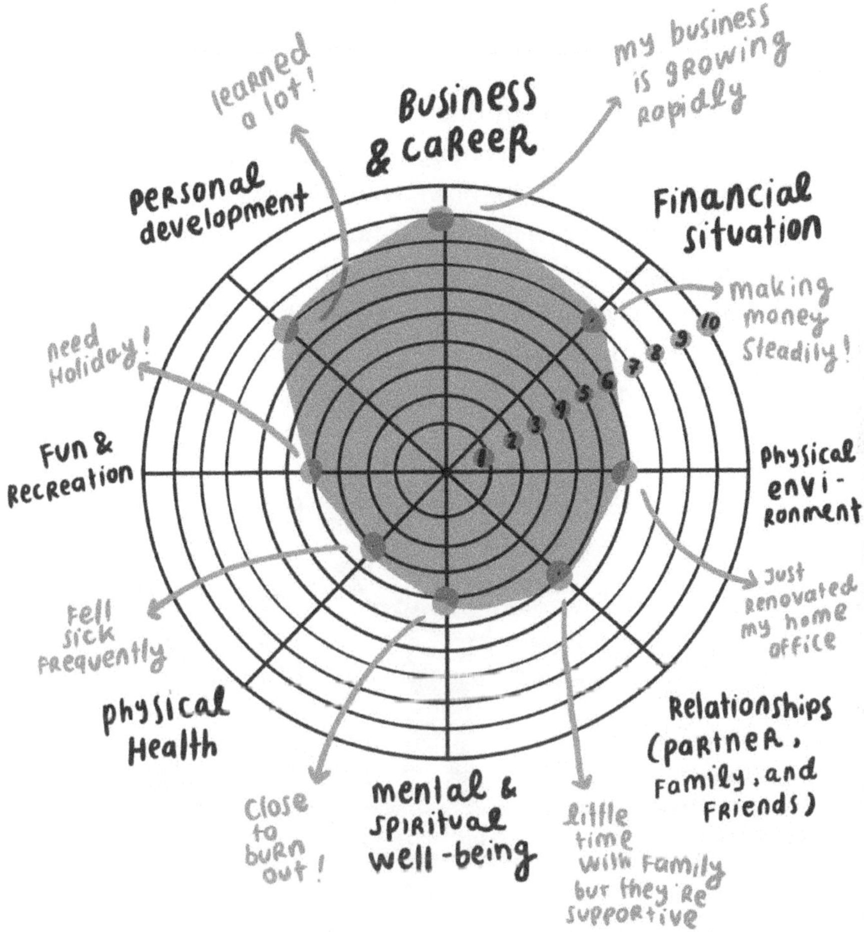

Now you may see it better, which life aspects you need to prioritize taking care of right now ☺

How would you feel about riding a vehicle with such a shape? This might be a good answer when someone asks, 'How are you, really?'

This tool helps us to assess and evaluate what aspects we want to improve and prioritize taking care of them now. Your business might be growing rapidly and looking terrific, but what about your health and mental well-being? Should you put exercise and getting enough sleep on a higher level of your priority and to-do list for now? What about your relationships with your closest ones? Are you happy about them? Do you want to improve this particular aspect?

Take a moment to think about your Wheel of Life. After that, you can work on the goal-setting journey for each aspect with the exercise sheet in the following chapter.

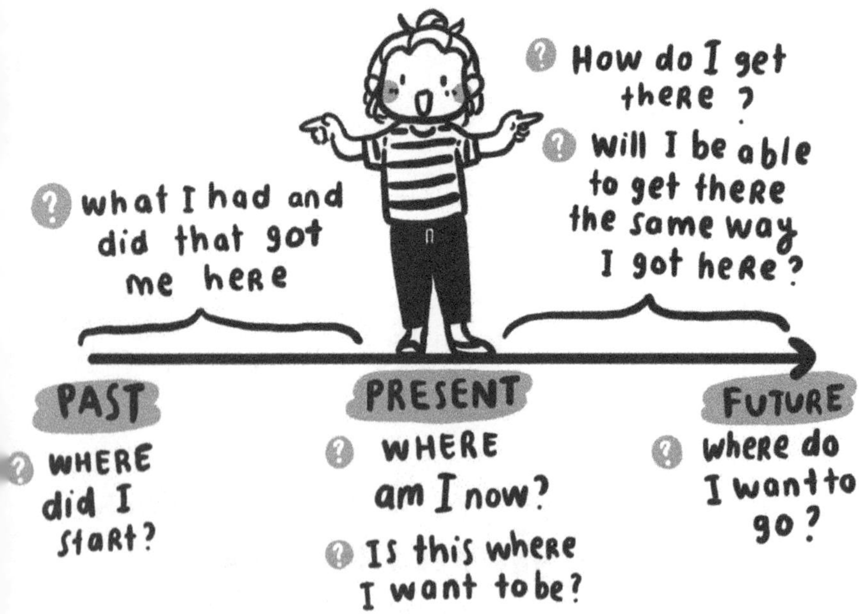

Exercise Template

Looking Forward to Looking Back!

After completing the 'Wheel of Life' exercise, use this table to help your goal-setting journey for each life aspect:

Life Aspect	
How important it is, based on my pyramid of values	
PRESENT	
Where am I now? (My score)	
Is this where I want to be? (Am I happy with my score?)	
PAST	
Where did I start? (Is my current score better than before?)	
What did I have and do that got me here?	
FUTURE	
Where do I want to go? (Do I want to get a better score? Or do I want to keep this one just like this and prioritize other aspects?)	
How do I get there? (What should I do to achieve it?)	
Will I be able to get there using the same way that got me here?	

It's a Big Dream, It's Also a Bunch of Tiny Sparks in Action

Many people find the question of 'What do you want to achieve in ten years?' or 'Where do you see yourself in twenty years?' very HR-like. Indeed, it's normal to think in a ten-year timeframe as a company employee, especially if the company has a decent career path system. On the other hand, in a personal context, we often still make our goals dream-like.

> I want to be successful and rich.
> I want to have bright children.
> I want to age gracefully.

The first step to gaining clarity on those goals is using the famous SMART framework. Turn your goal into something:

- **Specific:** Clear, well-defined, and unambiguous. *What exactly do you want to achieve?*
- **Measurable:** Has a straightforward way to track its progress. *How will you know when you've reached your goal?*
- **Achievable:** Ambitious but still realistic. *Reflect on your journey and consider your resources, skills, and limitations in the future.*
- **Relevant:** Aligns with your values, interests, and the bigger picture. *Does this goal matter to you in the long run?*
- **Time-phased:** Has a specific deadline or timeframe for completion. *When do you want to achieve this goal?*

Career and business-wise, in ten years, I want to grow my apparel business by opening five branches across the country.

When having a big goal feels scary and over—whelming ...
Shift your perspective, slice the big goal into smaller chunks, and deal with them one by one.
1 2 3 4 5 6 7 8 9 10 11 12
1 STEP AT A TIME

Family-wise, in fifteen years, I want my children to get into an Ivy League university.

Physical health and finance-wise, in twenty years, I want to be healthy and fit, even after retirement, and still be able to travel around the world.

After turning the goals into SMART goals, they may sound grand and ambitious yet feel far. We likely get overwhelmed by the scope. The amount of what needs to be done can feel paralysing and makes it hard to know where to begin. So, the next step is, instead of seeing each of them as one overwhelming goal, to *break it down into smaller chunks so that they can be carried out as measurable actions in shorter milestones*. This allows you to make a goal map and makes progress feel more manageable.

Here is a quick example:

Main goal: In ten years, I want to grow my apparel business, opening five branches across the country.

Life aspect: Business and career

- **Next year**: Build a solid foundation, develop a clear strategy for the brand identity, marketing strategy, and operations in the first branch, including human capital and inventory management system.
- **Next two years**: Prepare for growth by securing funding for expansion, and develop a standardized operational system, including human capital (recruitment and termination).
- **Next five years**: Open an additional two branches that solidify the brand identity, replicating successful strategies from the first branch.
- **Next ten years**: Maintaining the business while adding another two branches.

NEW YEAR RESOLUTION
» to be healthier
SPECIFIC
→ Jogging Regularly
MEASURABLE
→ 2 times a week
ACHIEVABLE
→ Jog not sprint...
RELEVANT
TIME PHASED
→ until December

Please be reminded that the process of turning a big dream into concrete, sliced actionable items takes work. Big consulting firms are paid a lot for this kind of exercise! Take some time to think it over and discuss with the people who will participate in it. Do you want to grow your business? While it comes from a personal ambition, do talk to your business partner. Admitting your children to Ivy League universities? Don't forget to talk to your spouse.

Align your intentions, and align your actions because teamwork definitely makes the dream work!

Exercise Template

Simple Goal Mapping

There are numerous ways to structure our goals. The framework presented here is just one example. The fundamental concept is to arrange all the goals according to different aspects of life (dimensions) in a sequential manner on a timeline. You can also use colours to indicate the order of priority. The exercise sheet on the next page is a guide, but feel free to adapt the aspects of life you wish to include and the timing for milestones based on your preferences. This flexibility is designed to empower you in your journey.

If you find yourself struggling with this, it's totally okay. Thinking about different aspects of your life and what you want to do about them can be overwhelming, as is the process of slicing a big dream into time-phased actions.

This exercise can be a catalyst for serious contemplation about your future. What you write today might look very different from what you'd write next year. We all make plans and decisions based on the information available to us, so *the aim is not to bind you to the same goal for decades, but to refine your current direction*. This process of adaptation and learning is what will guide you to make better decisions and plans for yourself in the future, instilling a sense of encouragement and motivation.

For example, if you say that career-wise you want to be in the C-level of a company ten years from now, you need to pursue a master's degree within the next five years and get a scholarship in the next two years to do so. If you try and fail to get a scholarship, you may start thinking about having a side hustle to finance it personally. The point is that you'll test your strategy and discover something about yourself.

simple goal-mapping

timeline →

Life aspect	NEXT YEAR	NEXT 2 YEARS	NEXT 5 YEARS	NEXT 10 YEARS
business & career				
Financial situation				
Family & Relationship				
personal development				
mental & spiritual well-being				
physical Health				

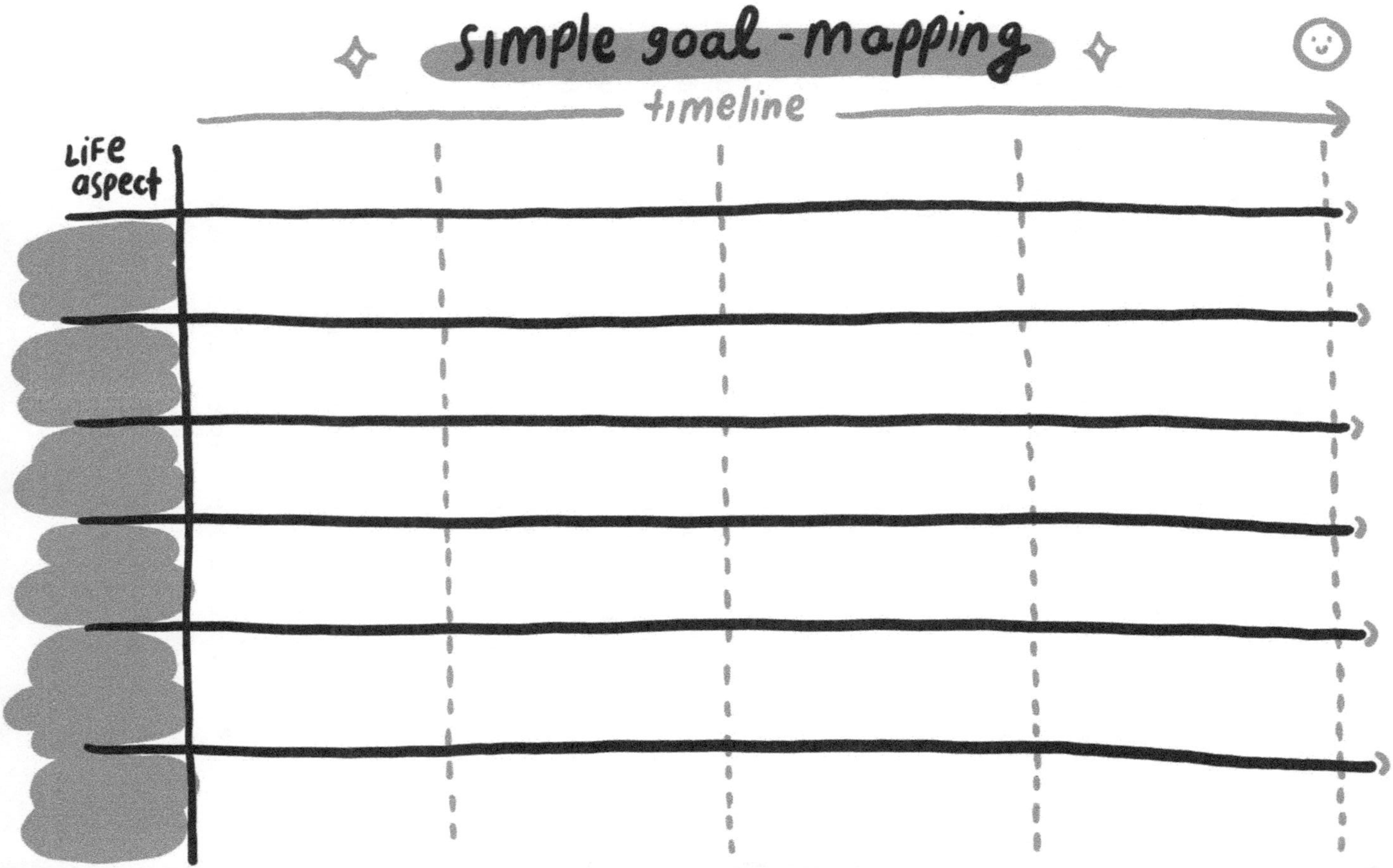
simple goal-mapping
timeline
LIFE aspect

Beyond 'Me': Goals and Relationships

While your goal map is about your journey, your relationships with people around you should be something to consider. If you are an entrepreneur, you might want to talk about your goals and plans with your business partner and team. If you have an ambitious career plan, you should discuss it with your spouse, especially if you have kids. If you want to be fit and healthy, you may also talk to people you're sharing meals with, your family, or your friends who are also your drinking buddies.

On the other hand, your goal map will also help you to gain clarity about your relationships in life. For example, if you plan to get married, then the goal will help you to decide what kind of partner you want to live your life with. Do you want to get married to a person who is against women having careers and who requires them to be homemakers? Do you want to have a business partner who wants to grow the business exponentially, with all the risks involved?

At the end of the day, your goals are yours, but the journey doesn't have to be a solo one. Sharing your goals with the right people can foster support, spark new ideas, and hold you accountable. Be the right person, find the right ones.

Self-Improved Me Note

Not everybody is used to being open about what they want, let alone sharing their goal maps. Here are some tips for bringing up this kind of discussion:

- **Choose the right time**, a good time when you are relaxed and can expect not to be interrupted. Avoid bringing it up during stressful situations.
- **Tailor your approach** based on your discussion partner's communication style. Be concise and clear for

your dreams, goals, and aspirations
your relationships and references

a more analytical partner or paint a more vivid picture if they're emotionally driven. Consider using visual aids, charts, mind maps, or vision boards to share your goals.

- **Be open to listening with the intention of aligning.** Ask for their feedback and ideas. Pay attention to their concerns.
- **Seek support and celebrate together**. Set milestones and plan to celebrate the achievements together. This reinforces the importance of your goals and strengthens your connection.
- **Plan and make time for evaluation and reflection later.**

Is Less Always More? Goals vs Focus

Goal setting is a powerful tool, but it can be a double-edged sword. Mapping our goals makes us realize there are many things that we'd like to achieve. In a way, it can be a reminder for us to focus more on working on them. At the same time, without managing our expectations, it can be burdensome. Goals in different life aspects might have conflicting demands on our time and energy. It is hard to focus on all of them simultaneously. For example, you may write down that you want more quality time with your family or personal development, but at the same time, your goal to get better physical health demands that you allocate regular time to the gym.

How do we navigate this? The first one is *prioritization*. Focus on one or two areas at a time. You can start with what you think is related to the most important values, especially if it's the non-negotiables (Check chapter 'Uncovering Your Inner Compass'). For example, if you think health is one of the most non-negotiables, you may put working out consistently as the top priority.

PRIORITIZATION

Integration

You can also sort your goals based on *urgency*—what requires immediate action. If you used the Wheel of Life (Check chapter 'Wheel of Life—Start With The Present') to reflect on how you feel about your life aspects today, you may check which one you rate the lowest. Imagine that the one scoring the lowest was 'financial situation'. Even though you said that money and wealth are not the most essential things in life, they are still worth your attention when you're not doing so well financially.

Besides prioritization, you may also try to find common threads and *integrate* some goals through the same action. Look for ways your goals in different areas can complement each other. For example, a health goal of exercise would increase your energy, which can support a career goal by building stamina during a challenging project. The health goal may also support the relationship aspect of your life when it is translated into exercising together with your partner.

Focusing on

your priorities

my battle is between ME and my goals!
i'm going through the path I've decided

CHAPTER 5

FOCUSING ON YOUR PRIORITIES

Is Work–Life Balance a Myth?

Many people are starting to say that work–life balance is a myth. When we say balance, the image of a scale or a seesaw may come to mind. We think that it is about finding the right formula for dividing your time between work and your personal life fairly. Some believe that since there are only twenty-four hours per day and we need about six to eight hours to sleep, we should just split the rest (fourteen to eighteen hours) fifty-fifty between work and personal life.

However, work–life balance can be perceived more like dancing on a ball while juggling many other balls with your hands and feet. These balls represent your different responsibilities: work tasks, family needs, personal health, hobbies, etc. Every day, we try hard not to let any of the balls slip, and to do that, we have to keep moving and maintain the dynamics with different positions and poses. Just like cycling, you must keep moving to keep the balance, only it's harder. Especially if you have more goals, you'll have even more commitments and responsibilities.

life Balance

WHAT IS OFTEN PERCEIVED :

WHAT IT ACTUALLY IS :

A balanced life may also look different. There will be days where having a work–life balance means taking days off of work to watch your children's school performances. Still, on other days, it means outsourcing laundry and catering services to take care of your family because you need to go on a business trip.

Everybody dances and juggles differently, but please remember to be kind to yourself, too. Be aware of your limitations. *Sometimes we mess up, and dropping a ball occasionally is inevitable.*

That's okay!

Guilt Management on Deciding What Is Urgent and Important

While juggling, it is important to decide what to keep juggling and what to let go. As women, we are often expected to take care of a lot of things at the same time. It is worsened by the stereotype that women are better multitaskers than men (Szameitat, 2015). However, research from the Institute of Psychology at Aachen University in Germany busted this myth. Women are not better at multitasking than men (Hirsch, 2019).

The problem is that the stereotypes and the expectations accompanying them often make us feel guilty when we can't handle everything. I still remember how my mom would get annoyed every time we returned from holiday because she had to take care of us, the kids, the dirty laundry we brought from the holiday, and the house. We would offer to help, but she always told us that we should sit still because there was a chance that we would mess up and double the burden. Now that I am a mother myself, I can relate to what she felt back then, but

I have learned that it's better to have my priorities sorted, let go of some things, and let my family chill.

A method commonly used for prioritizing is the Eisenhower Matrix, a table where we categorize things on our to-do list into the following categories: urgent vs not urgent, important vs not important. The Eisenhower Matrix can be a powerful tool for helping us focus on the first thing first.

Quadrant One: Do It Now (Urgent and Important)

These tasks demand immediate attention and can't be put off. For example, as a mom, this might include taking care of a sick child. Or at work, it might be an upcoming deadline for the BOD report.

Quadrant Two: Schedule It (Important But Not Urgent)

These are important tasks that contribute to our long-term goals but don't require immediate action. For example, working out at the gym or joining a course that will upgrade your skills at work.

Quadrant Three: Delegate It (Urgent But Not Important)

These tasks are time-sensitive but don't necessarily require your expertise. Consider delegating them to free up your time for more important things. For example, grocery shopping or preparing for your boss's farewell party (let the interns be creative!)

Quadrant four: Eliminate It (Not Urgent and Not Important)

These tasks can be eliminated from your list altogether. They don't contribute to your well-being or your family's needs. For example—surprise, surprise—excessive social media scrolling.

the Famous Eisenhower Matrix

Some notes we need to keep in mind: As our work–life balance is dynamic, this matrix should be reviewed and adjusted regularly. What is categorized as urgent today might be categorized differently tomorrow.

Another thing is that the matrix can be very subjective. For example, as a working mom, cooking is something that I would happily delegate, either to my assistant or a food delivery service. However, for mothers whose kids require special diets, it becomes crucial. Or social media scrolling. If you are working as a social media intelligence consultant, that would be something you put on the first quadrant.

Therefore, please manage your guilt. There are times when we put our loved ones' needs on the not-important quadrant, but this doesn't mean that we're neglectful or not responsible. What's important and urgent for you will likely differ from the others.

Be efficient, and don't procrastinate urgent things.

Don't feel bad when you have to postpone and reschedule some tasks.

Don't feel guilty when you delegate.

Don't indulge yourself and make excuses for things you should eliminate.

Self-Improved Me Note

Practice makes progress. Try using the Eisenhower Matrix as your weekly or monthly prioritization framework. Arrange your to-do list inside the table and check if you can commit to what is written.

Delegation Is a Discipline

Managing our guilt of being unable to handle everything or to be present for everything is one problem that arises when we stick to our priorities and delegate. Perfectionism might be another one. While being a perfectionist is still often seen in a positive light, it reflects some deeper issues like fear of failure, a result-oriented mindset, the inability to set realistic standards, and some selfishness.

It hit me hard when I read Ryan Holiday's book, *Discipline Is Destiny: The Power of Self-Control* and got another perspective to perfectionism.

'What was it? Was it humility? An obsession with getting the little things right? No, those are the reassuring excuses we make for what is a kind of narcissism and obsession. We're convinced that everyone cares so much about what we're doing that we get stuck. We tell ourselves it's self-discipline when in fact, it's self-consciousness.'

I realize that it is not easy for some of us to delegate things. Being able to delegate requires the humility to let go of some things and seek help; to cooperate, to rely on, and trust the other. It is also about shifting your mindset to a growth mindset, to let failures happen, and be open to the learning process.

At the end of the day, delegation is a discipline and needs to be practised constantly, so it becomes easier to handle.

Self-Improved Me Note

When it feels hard for you to delegate, think about what the worst thing is that can happen if you delegate the task. What is the worst that can happen if you ask your partner to do grocery shopping? Maybe they will buy the wrong detergent brand or forget to grab the soy sauce. Would that be so bad?

INABILITY
TO
delegate

unrealistic standards...
Selfishness
(I have to control everything)
FEAR of Failure; Fixed mindset
Result Oriented
INABILITY
to
delegate

Time Management Is a Resource Trade-Off

Just like work–life balance, time management is another topic that people are constantly wondering about. How do we do it? Is it even possible?

Time management is often thought to be about how we manage the twenty-four hours in a day. However, it's more about how you manage your resources: time, money, and energy—both physical and mental. You can earn money with your time but you can also save time with your money. For example, you can just order your lunch and get it delivered with some additional cost. The time you'd spend cooking and preparing lunch would instead be used to work on a commercial project.

Not limited to money and time, your resources also include your energy and focus. For example, driving is something that doesn't spark joy for my father and takes more energy than other tasks. So, he prefers paying someone to do it for him because with a similar amount of energy, he can work on something more profitable or enjoyable.

Think of your resources as something quantifiable so it's easier for you to manage them, especially when you need to identify what's worth it and what isn't.

An important note: Seeing time management as a resource trade-off and asking, 'What will we get in return? Is it worth it?' doesn't necessarily mean we become materialistic per se. It doesn't have to give us material gain. It can be a stronger relationship with your loved ones (priceless!), it can be a sense of joy, pursuing passions, or a purely altruistic reward as long as it aligns with our values and priorities. *The true reward isn't just about productivity, but about achieving what matters most to us.*

Take a deep breath, assess your resources, and start crafting your ideal day—one mindful trade-off at a time.

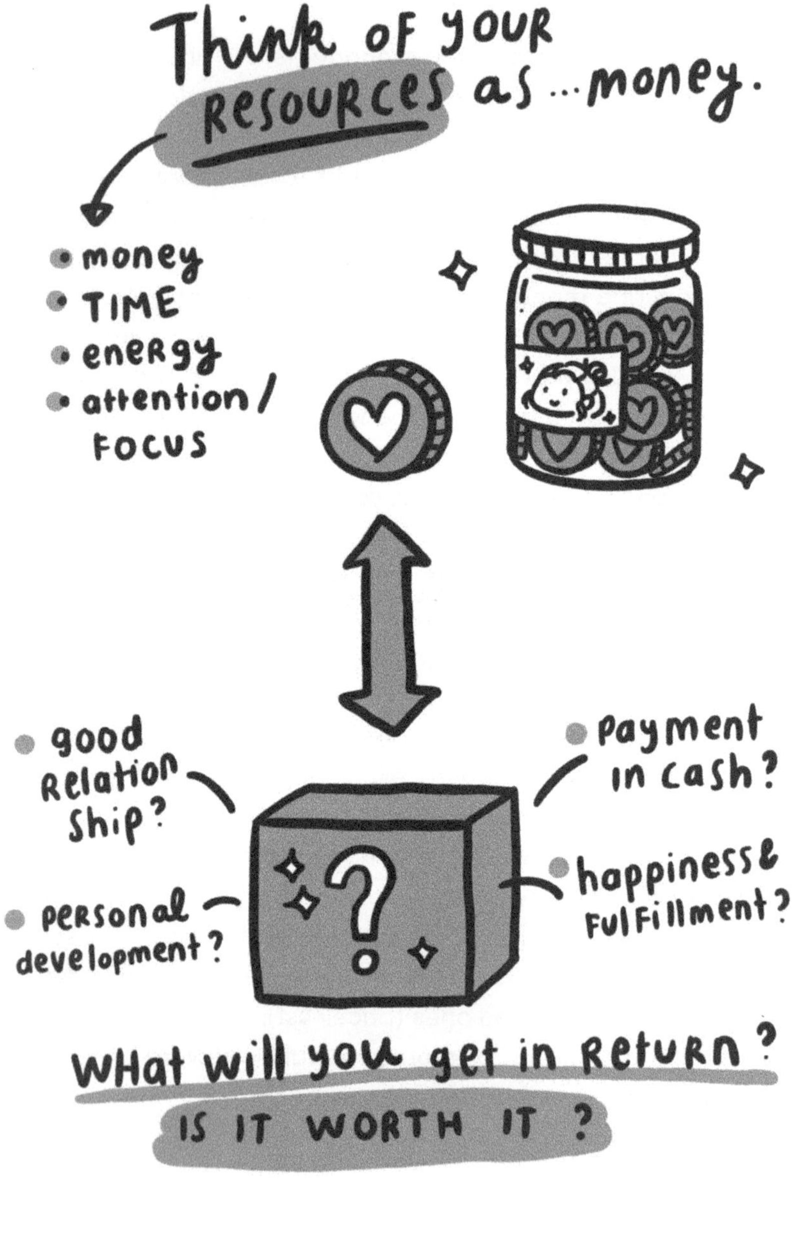
Think of your resources as ... money.
money
TIME
energy
attention/ focus
good Relationship?
Payment in cash?
personal development?
happiness & fulfillment?
?
WHat will you get in Return?
IS IT WORTH IT ?

When it comes to resource management for productivity, the two questions should be:

'What do I get in return?'

'What does it cost me?'

What Does 'Expensive' Cost?

In return for our time, money, and energy, we may receive happiness and better well-being. On the other hand, some things may cost our well-being or even our sanity.

Once, I ordered some clothes for my son online. The service was terrible, and I received a design different from what I had ordered. Since the transaction was not on an e-commerce platform but from a customer to a seller, I had to complain directly to the seller. Their response was so unprofessional that I got terribly annoyed. They eventually told me to ship the item back and promised to send the right thing. After I returned the item, I didn't hear anything from them. After many reproachful messages, they finally told me they couldn't replace it because the condition of the item didn't meet their exchange policy. I got furious and felt scammed. As someone active on social media, I couldn't help but complain and share this experience with my audience.

At one point, I realized that I had spent too much time on a transaction that had cost me only about $20. Instead of getting annoyed about it, messaging the seller, and venting on social media, I could've worked on something else that was worth it.

People are often very careful with money because it's a tangible resource. Well-being and sanity, while harder to quantify, are equally valuable and have a significant impact. Concentrating on complex projects is easier when your mind is not irked by something else (e.g., a rude online seller).

HOW I UNDERSTAND EXPENSIVENESS as I grow older

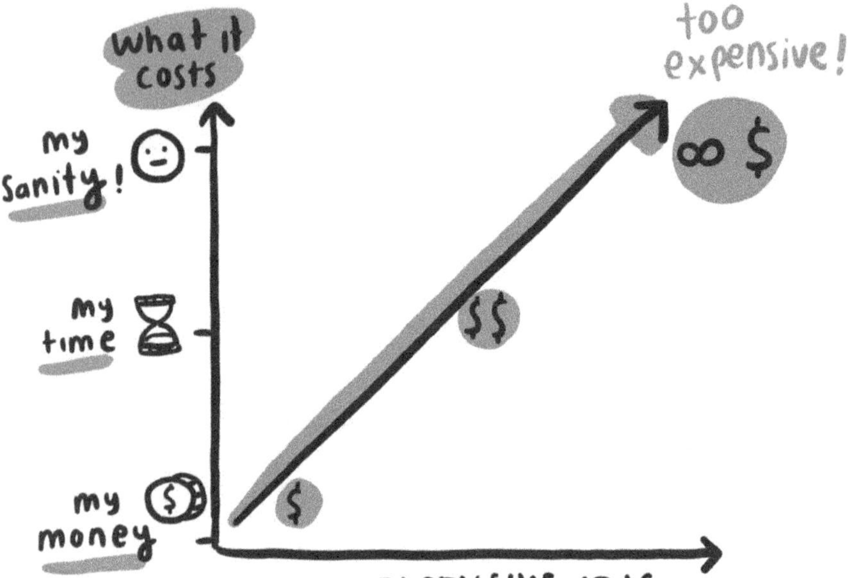

This also affected my mood and how I responded to my kid. Nothing is more expensive than something that costs us our sanity!

It may take practice but adopting the mindset that 'nothing is more expensive than something that costs us our sanity' empowers us to make conscious choices and stick to our priorities.

Self-Improved Me Note

When dealing with a problem that could potentially cost your sanity, practise taking a deep breath and asking yourself, 'What is the best scenario that I'm expecting? Is that even possible? Is it worth it?'

Every Time You Say 'Yes' to Something, You Say 'No' to Something Else

One thing we don't often realize is that we spend too much time on things that don't matter just because we cannot say no to them.

We often find ourselves stretched thin, overwhelmed by commitments we regret. The culprit behind this? Our inability to say no and a problem establishing boundaries. Here are some possible causes of this problem and some things you can do to navigate them:

1. Fear of disapproval

The fear of disapproval can be a powerful reason not to say no. We worry about disappointing others or jeopardizing relationships. Imagine you have an important deadline in two days. Then your boyfriend's sister asks you to accompany her for some shopping and a coffee afterward.

Remember that every time you say 'YES' to something...

You're saying 'NO' to something else...

sometimes without realizing it.

You would like to decline, but you're afraid you'll hurt her. So you say yes and have to work extra hard a day before the deadline.

While it's okay to compromise sometimes, you should let this be an exception, not the rule, because true connections are built on mutual understanding and respect. Communicating our boundaries clearly is a way to foster healthier relationships where 'no' isn't seen as a rejection but as a form of respect to both parties.

2. Desire and attachment to an identity

Another hurdle is our attachment to a particular identity. We might feel obligated to say yes to tasks that align with an image we've created for ourselves, even if it no longer resonates with our current priorities. For example, you can't say no when someone from your non-profit community asks you to be part of the fundraising committee because you've always been the one to convince people to become donors. You can't say no because you're attached to your identity: the convincing one, the nice one, the one who contributes to the community.

While having this desire and attachment is normal, you can remind yourself that growth requires room for new things and opportunities. Saying no allows us to explore, experience new things, and redefine who we are. Just because we say no to being a fundraising committee member, it doesn't mean that we're not nice or not contributing to society anymore. To ease this feeling, be aware that identity is not static, and change is necessary to maintain authenticity.

3. Fear of missing out

The fear of missing out can be paralysing; sometimes, it's mixed with our attachment to an identity.

You can't say no to party invitations because you've always been the 'it' girl on the VIP list. You don't want to decline because you want to show up and show that you are still relevant. You want to catch up and be there. This might become a problem when other commitments need your attention and time. Maybe now you have roles with more responsibilities at the office, or perhaps you have a partner and kids.

I once listened to Ryan Holiday's podcast on Google Talks ('Stillness is the Key', Ryan Holiday), and he gave an incredible practical tip to navigate this fear of missing out: When you want to say yes to something because you're afraid to say no, imagine vividly who you take that time and energy from.

For example, when you say yes to an office event on the weekend, imagine what you're saying no to: it could be your family, the time to catch up with old friends, or your rest day.

Because every time you say yes to something, you actually say no to something else.

When Inspiration Becomes Distraction

There's a saying attributed to Abraham Lincoln: 'If I had eight hours to chop down a tree, I'd spend six hours sharpening my axe.' This saying highlights the importance of preparation. However, in today's world, overflowing with inspiration, the act of planning and preparation can become a form of procrastination itself. It should be called 'the paradox of planning'. It is no longer a matter of time management or resource management. No matter how sharp the axe is, no trees will ever be chopped down if it's only sharpened and unused.

SELF-REWARD
Acceptance of Missing out
FROM me
TO me

But when will you start working on a project?
I'm still finding ideas and inspirations here
Bag of Ideas and inspiration
bag of more ideas and inspiration

The root of this problem could be our fear of imperfection. We get tangled in an endless loop of planning, researching, and refining, paralysed by our desire to get it 'just right'. This fear prevents us from executing the inspiration, from cooking it into work.

To avoid this trap, there are some things you should remind yourself:

- **Execution is king:** Ideas are valuable, but their true worth lies in their implementation, so . . .
- **Start with a small step**: Take your first action and let the first small result be a part of the further development stage. Don't be afraid of messing up. How bad can it be? Because anyway . . .
- **Done is better than perfect:** You can't learn from something that is not finished. The more you try, the more you learn because . . .
- **Quantity breeds quality:** Be bold and generate a large volume of ideas, even if they seem rough initially. The brainstorming process itself can spark unexpected connections and lead to hidden gems. Creating something is indeed about connecting the dots, but you have to collect the dots first!

In short, let's get started now!

"Inspiration is for
AMATEURS. The rest of us
just show up and get to
WORK. If you wait around
for the clouds to part and
a bolt of lightning to
strike you in
the brain, you
are not going
to make an awful
lot of WORK. All
the best ideas come
out of the process;
they come out of
the work itself."
–Chuck Close

CUT HERE TO CLAIM a little reward FOR yourself

to
DO
DO
DO
list
and
beyond!

CHAPTER 6

TO DO-DO-DO LIST AND BEYOND!

Exercise Template

Design Your Day, Your Way

Besides goals and priorities, designing our schedule plan can be more effective when we are aware of ourselves and our energy levels. Try to figure these out:

- **Morning lark or night owl?** When are you most focused and alert? Schedule the hardest or the most demanding tasks for your peak energy hours.
- **Fuel for focus:** Do coffee breaks and snacks help your concentration or create distractions? Plan your schedule accordingly. If you work best when fuelled, schedule those energy boosters alongside demanding tasks.
- **Cramming vs flow:** Do you thrive under pressure, or do last-minute deadlines leave you feeling panicked and unproductive? Schedule creative tasks for times when your mind is naturally flowing and leave room for buffer time on deadlines if you need a more structured approach.
- **Social battery recharge:** Do you need time to unwind after social interaction? Block out 'quiet time' after meetings or phone calls to recharge your social battery and avoid burnout.

understand your energy level

? do you find it easier to work during the day or late at night?

? Do coffee and snack breaks help you focus / regain your focus?

? are you okay to do things at the last minute before deadlines? Is it good for the flow of your creative juice?

? do you need days to recharge your social battery?

Building Your Ideal Schedule

Once you understand your energy patterns better, start experimenting with your schedule. For example:

Time	Energy Level	Type of Tasks
Morning	High	Analytical work
Mid-Morning	Energy Dip	Coffee break + snack, light stretching Administrative work like catching up on emails
Afternoon	Moderate	Tasks that require less cognitive effort like reviewing materials
Late Afternoon	Energy Dip	Another short break Schedule meetings or collaborative tasks that require less individual focus
Evening	Low	Light routine tasks Hobbies and interests, e.g., reading a book

Try different schedules until you find what works best for you. Adjust as needed because your energy levels might fluctuate. Befriend the current and surf your energy waves!

TIME vs Energy Level Check

Time	Energy LVL	Suitable task type

Tips

Buffer More to Suffer Less

Do you hate Mondays? Do you despair before going back to work or school after the holidays?

The gap between holidays (especially if they were long!) and working days (especially if you're commuting for hours) makes it even more difficult for us to return to work. It feels scary, like jumping from a cliff, or it might feel like climbing some very steep stairs.

Try to prepare and do one or two things on the next day's to-do list. For example, review your calendar, draft responses to urgent emails that need to be answered the following morning, tidy up your working space, pre-prepare your kids' lunch, or plan your outfit (hello, ladies!). This will save you time in the morning, make the transition smoother, and allow you to begin working on the most demanding tasks as early as possible.

I Hate monday
Sunday
MONDay

okay, let's add another step FOR easieR tRansition
Sunday
do one oR two things in advance to make your Monday easieR: clean youR desk, get youR to-do-list ready, dRaft some email Responses,
monday PReparation
MONDay

Tips

Start with a Win!

For a productivity boost, *tackle a quick and easy task on your to-do list first*. Checking it off triggers a dopamine hit, giving you a surge of confidence to do the following, more challenging item. This momentum helps you power through your most demanding tasks while your energy is still high.

to-do list hack!

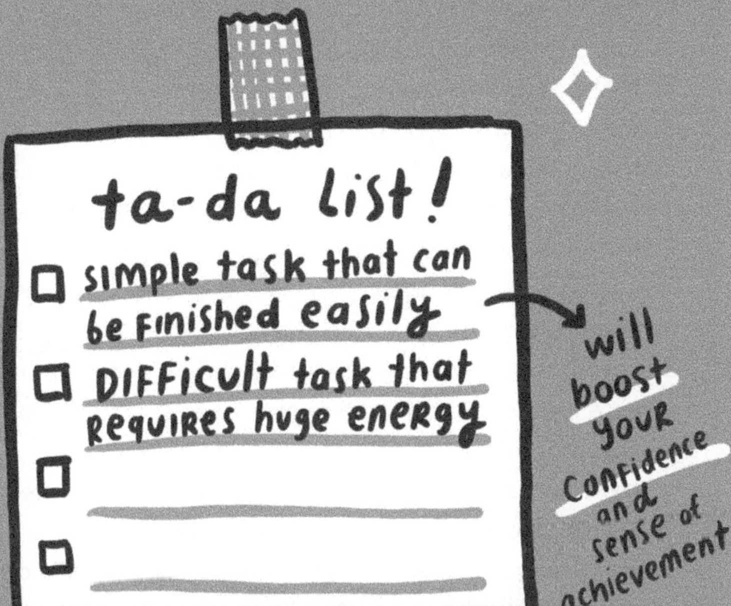

Do Your Best, Do Your Rest

In our fast-paced lives, we may feel guilty about doing less. We might believe that rest equates to laziness or wasted time, a burden on our ever-growing to-do lists. However, rest is vital to keep our engines running, allowing us to return to our tasks with renewed focus, creative juice, and resilience. *It's not easy to unlearn and instil the mindset that rest isn't the antithesis of work; and instead, it is its essential partner*. Especially if you usually have hundreds of things to do on busy days. Your mind will be restless when you don't do anything.

I feel this as a mother. Motherhood is perceived and (often glorified) as a job that doesn't have a holiday. Some people say that mothers can't get sick days, so they have to be healthy even when they are not. When a mother chooses me-time or goes on holiday without her kids, people ask, 'How can you be so selfish and leave them?' This should not be normalized because mothers, like everyone else, need rest to recharge and function properly.

And as author Alex Soojung-Kim Pang discusses in his book *Rest*, rest is something that we need to work for, 'Rest is not something that the world gives us. It's never been a gift. It's never been something you do when you've finished everything else. If you want rest, you have to take it. You have to resist the lure of busyness, make time for rest, take it seriously, and protect it from a world that is intent on stealing it.'

So, how do we shift our mindset and embrace the power of rest?

Why planning time to REST is good FOR US ...

gaining Happiness while looking forward to it = Longer Lasting Happiness

Avoiding impulsive decision because we feel that we don't get what we deserve.

time to prepare and ensure smooth transition

compare your plan with its fully realized version so you may plan better in the future

Understand the Benefits

A well-rested mind is sharper, more creative, and better at problem-solving. It fosters emotional resilience, allowing us to navigate challenges with greater calm and perspective. This also affects our relationship with our loved ones as we're more easily irritated when we are tired and lack sleep. Additionally, rest strengthens our physical health, boosting our immune system and reducing stress-related illnesses. With all these benefits, we should reframe rest, not as something selfish but as a part of our effort to take care of ourselves so we can better care for others.

Schedule It! Put It on Your To-Do List!

Think of rest as a non-negotiable appointment, just like a crucial work meeting. Schedule time in your calendar, just as you would any other commitment. This act of planning demonstrates the importance you place on your well-being. Just like completing a task, put a checkmark on your to-do list. Acknowledge the positive impact it has on your productivity and overall well-being.

Experiment and Find What Works for You

Rest is a personal journey. What works for one person might not work for another. Experiment with different ways and identify what rejuvenates you the most. Rest is not only limited to sleep (arguably the most important, though); it may also come through meditation, spending time in nature, disconnecting from electronics, or simply doing nothing at home. Evaluate what works for you for better planning in the future.

do you exercise ?
well, I'm a member of a gym !
my member card :
GYM MEMBERSHIP
DONOR
ID NO : 080989999
expiry : -*
* (never came anyway...)

So, if any mother is reading this, repeat after me, 'Me time is not selfish; I'm doing it for my family!' That's legit.

Self-Improved Me Note

Let's take some action! Grab your calendar and do the following:

- Make a commitment to sleep at least seven hours and try to stick with it for at least a week.
- Schedule a day off this month and think about what kind of fun and recreational activities you want to do that day. Planning to do nothing is excellent, too!

Self-Discipline is Self-Love

'Oh, after all the deadlines and this project wrapped, I deserve a #selfreward. I'm taking that holiday trip I can't afford! But YOLO!'

'Oh, I'm not going to the gym anymore! Who cares about a flat stomach and skinny arms? I'm getting the donut instead. I love my body the way it is, and this is #selflove.'

'Self-love' is often equated with 'self-indulgence', which then becomes an excuse for making unwise and self-destructive decisions: buying things you don't need with money you don't have, robbing your own emergency fund for an impulsive holiday, or procrastinating because you don't want to deal with the discomfort (then panicking a day before the deadline).

Love comes in many forms and doesn't always bring instant comfort. If your child wants to skip school because they do not feel comfortable with math exams, would you allow it because you love them? If your best friend wants to cheat on their spouse because they don't find comfort in their current relationship, would you support it? You may say no because you are in a

Self-DISCIPLINE
IS
SELFLOVE
and
self-
Reward
is not
self-
indulgence.

position with perspectives to see far enough into the future to realize that these are terrible decisions for the future.

However, when making decisions for ourselves, we are prone to bias.

So, how do we tell the difference between self-love and self-indulgence?

Self-indulgence is a short-term fix. It focuses on instant gratification, fulfilling desires in the moment, often without considering the consequences. This leads to unsustainable actions, which might feel good in the short term but ultimately lead to negative consequences. It doesn't address deeper needs or contribute to our overall well-being. For example, the unbudgeted holiday you pay with your credit card may get you instant happiness (and cool Instagram content), but the pressure of paying it off later may cost you your future well-being.

On the other hand, self-love is the foundation for long-term growth. Self-loving actions should benefit you in the long run, even if they don't bring immediate comfort. It requires self-discipline, for example, eating healthy, getting enough sleep, exercising regularly, and setting goals that challenge you.

The key is to find a balance and remember that self-discipline is self-love. You may listen to your needs and desires, but also be mindful of the long-term consequences that may conflict with your goals and current progress. Self-love is about creating a sustainable and fulfilling life for yourself.

Self-Improved Me Note

Reflect on your past self-love and self-reward actions that you have taken in the past three months. Could they be self-indulgence in disguise?

12
9
3
6
the greatest
freedom
comes from
the greatest
strictness
Paul Valéry

Success Is a Boring Process That Works

We are all familiar with the motivational quote, 'To succeed, be prepared to fail.'

But there's another truth about success that is less talked about—it's often *boring*. While failure can be dramatic and material for a podcast that people can talk about later, boredom never sounds romantic. Boredom doesn't bear the zero-to-hero narrative. It's zero to one, one to one-and-a-half before getting to two. Boredom is an uneventful repetition.

Even after reaching what we thought we wanted to reach, we still have to deal with boredom. You still have to work, maybe even harder, once promoted to C-level. You still have to think about the next move once your business reaches the all-time-high revenue target. You still have to make even more content after your follower count reaches 100,000.

Success is boring because it's an ongoing process, not a summit we stop climbing after we arrive. It's fair to modify the quote in the first paragraph to: *'To succeed, be prepared to be bored.'*

So, how do we befriend boredom? Embrace the power of small wins. Acknowledge our progress, even the incremental improvements. Celebrate them. Find ways to be more mindful about small happiness in our routine and be grateful for it. In the end, the most fulfilling successes are often the ones where we savour the journey as much as the arrival.

what is visible and celebrated
the hard and BORING things that are too BORING for other people to notice.

Build a Routine, Celebrate the Small Wins

The constant task juggling can sometimes drive us crazy. However, there is a way to streamline our day without feeling overwhelmed by building routines.

Routines are more than just a set schedule; they are powerful tools that empower us to manage consistency and automate the habits that bring us closer to our goals. By turning 'shoulds' into 'autos', we can lighten our mental load and decision fatigue, leaving us more space for things that need more of our focus and energy.

Take a skincare routine, for example. We all know we need to be consistent to get results, but how often is it forgotten? By incorporating it into your routine, like embedding it between brushing your teeth and climbing into bed, you turn a chore into an automatic action. Over time, it becomes second nature.

We can also anchor our new routines to our existing ones or our routines to others'. For example, as a mother, you can utilize your child's school schedule as an anchor point. Maybe you take yoga classes right after they leave for school or dedicate a reading session for yourself while they're in tutoring. This reduces the mental burden of 'finding the time' and creates a natural transition into your new habit.

We can build routines out of any kind of habit, the ones that you enjoy or those you have to push into your schedule. Charles Duhigg, in his book *The Power of Habit*, explains the habit loop, which is a cycle of cue, routine, and reward.

For example, when you commit to your skincare ritual regularly (the routine), the reward might be a healthy glow or plumper skin (the reward). This positive reinforcement motivates you to continue the routine (the cue).

However, not all routines can bring immediate rewards. For example, you might want to build a habit of exercising

Creating good Habits*: Building a routine

Make it OBVIOUS

Keep the catalysts/ reminders visible

e.g. place a bottle of water on your nightstand so you see it first in the morning.

Make it Attractive

Make the process more engaging /Fun

e.g. Join a dance class as a part of your exercise routine

Make it EASY

try to remove the obstacles and break it down into simpler steps

e.g. aim to read 10 pages/day instead of 1 book/month

Make it SATISFYING

make a tracker to see your progress and celebrate your small wins!

*) Adapted from James Clear's *Atomic Habits* (2018)

consistently, but your aim is to maintain your physical health so that you can still be active when you're sixty. In this case, you can reward yourself for solely sticking to the routine, knowing that the long-term benefits are worth it.

In the best-selling book *Atomic Habits: An Easy & Proven Way to Build Good Habits & Break Bad Ones*, James Clear suggests making the process of building a habit satisfying by creating a tracker to mark your progress and consistency. This can be a reward that will be the cue, reinforcing the positive feedback loop and keeping us motivated.

Acknowledge the Progress, Honour the Process

Besides routine, another part of the habit loop to pay attention to is the 'reward'. While rewards are a powerful tool for building habits, celebrating the journey itself becomes even more crucial in the context of long-term goals. Each step, no matter how small, is a victory on the path to achieving your dreams. Acknowledging and tracking your progress as a series of mini-wins will keep you motivated and moving forward. It's a way to honour your process.

Looking back at your progress log reveals the ordinary but essential actions you take consistently. Your log becomes a tangible reminder of your consistency and breeds confidence, your belief in your ability to show up and progress towards your goal. Tracking your progress also helps you focus on your own goals, preventing distractions from the achievements of others. Your progress log is evidence of your personal growth story. So, the next time you see someone sharing their journey of losing weight with the before and after photos, you can just

Focusing on the Result
I didn't lose weight at all...

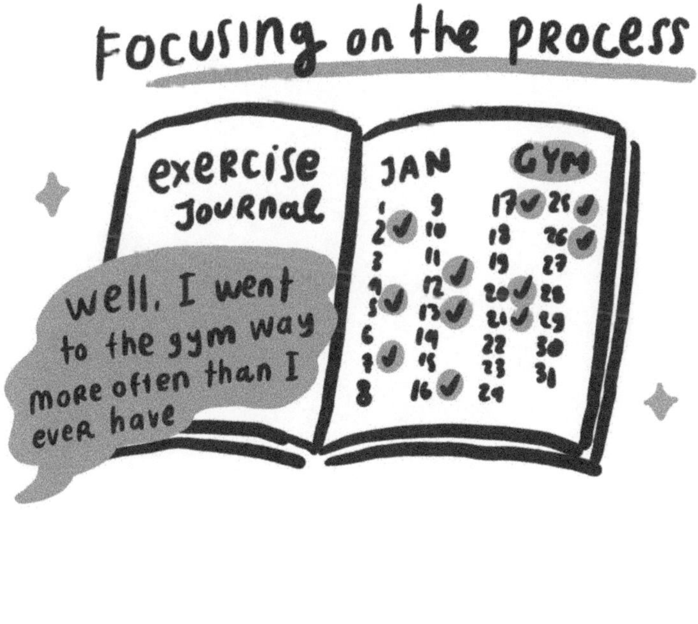
Focusing on the Process
exercise Journal
JAN
GYM
well, I went to the gym way more often than I ever have

check your progress tracker and remind yourself that you're already on track.

Shiny 'after' photos are great, but don't get blinded by someone else's highlight reel. Be proud of your progress tracker—it's your personal trophy case!

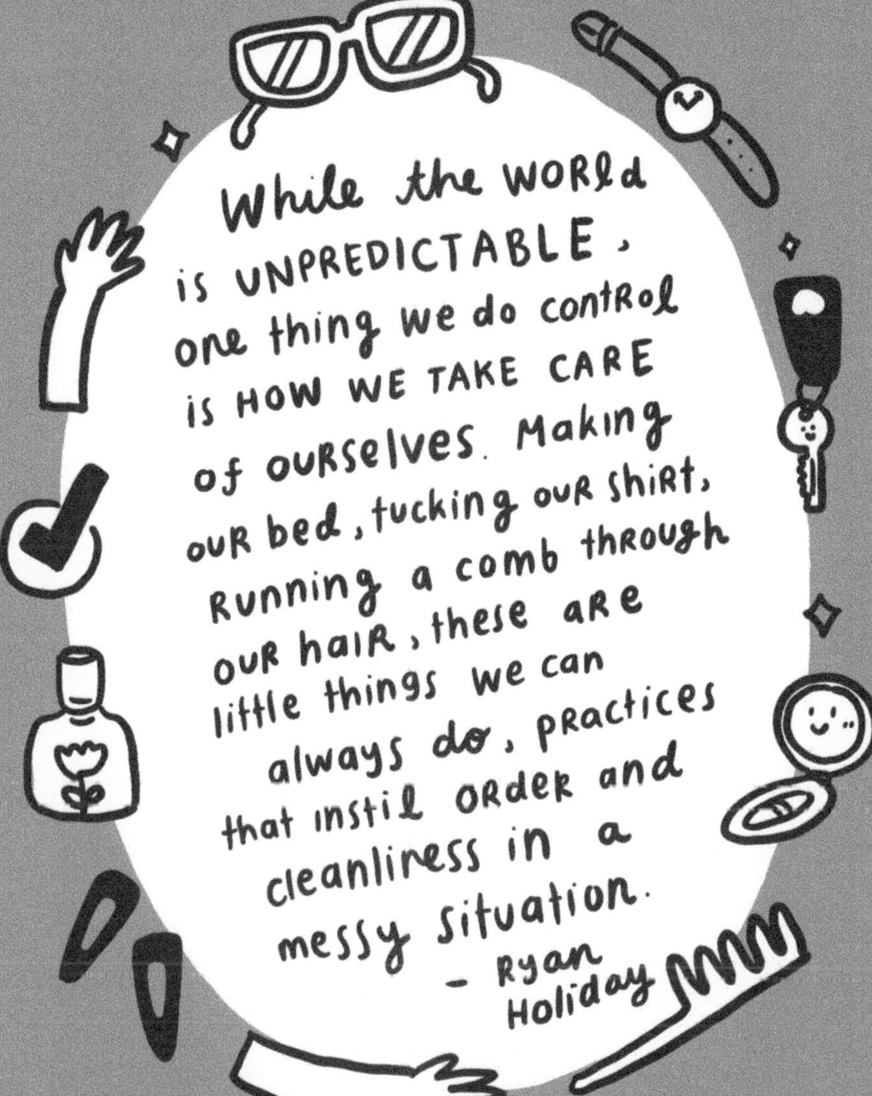
While the WORLD
is UNPREDICTABLE,
one thing we do control
is HOW WE TAKE CARE
of ourselves. Making
our bed, tucking our shirt,
Running a comb through
our hair, these are
little things we can
always do, practices
that instil order and
cleanliness in a
messy situation.
- Ryan
Holiday

small progress is still progress

CHAPTER 7

SMALL PROGRESS IS STILL PROGRESS

Journalling 101: Track Any Progress, Be Proud of Your Current Best

Journalling is a powerful way to track our progress, yet as technology advances, this act is not limited to just using books.

Beyond the pen and paper, here are some diverse ways to track your progress:

- **Digital ink:** Blogs, online journals, and note-taking apps like Evernote can be platforms to record your experiences and learnings.
- **Spreadsheets:** Perfect for data-driven individuals, spreadsheets allow you to track quantitative progress and analyse trends over time.
- **Voice memos:** Ideal for capturing spontaneous thoughts and ideas, voice recordings offer a personal touch to journalling.
- **Visual inspiration:** Create a video diary to document your progress visually, whether it's your fitness journey or artistic endeavours.
- **Specialized apps:** Leverage the power of purpose-built apps like Goodreads for book tracking, Strava for fitness goals, or Google Fit for general well-being.

tracking different progress

method	examples of use
 AUDIO/VISUAL RECORDING	» Artwork creation » Baking skill » Dancing routine
 Journalling	» habit tracking » bad habit tracking » Mood diary
 Spreadsheet	» Saving progress » Spending habit » Income from time to time
 Special apps	» exercise routine (google fit, strava) » Reading challenge (goodreads)

The Essential Ingredients

No matter the format, your progress journal should include these key elements:

- **Date and time:** Provide context for your entries and track your progress over time.
- **Activity notes:** Briefly describe the activity you're tracking.
- **Measurable data:** Include quantifiable data (like the number of pages read) or qualitative notes (like improvement in a skill) to assess your progress.

Remember to be aware of your preferences and behaviour. Choose a method that best suits your learning style and preferences. Don't get overwhelmed by fancy tools. The key is to find a system that works for you and consistently record your journey. For example, I love writing on paper, so I keep a journal and feel incomplete without hand writing my experience. On the other hand, my friend hates hand writing and loves practicality, so they use a note-taking app on their smartphone that comes in handy.

So, pick your method and celebrate your current best!

Self-Improved Me Note

Some people use the traditional method of bullet journalling digitally on their gadgets. Consider these:

- **Find the right app**: Explore different apps to find one that suits your needs and preferences. Consider features like customizable layouts, digital pens with pressure sensitivity, and sticker options.
- **Embrace the digital world**: While replicating the traditional pen-and-paper feel, feel free to get creative

with the digital tools. Use hyperlinks to connect related tasks, include some photos for documentation, web clippings for inspiration, and use colour-coding for better organization.

- **Maintain the core principles**: Even in a digital format, stick to the core bullet journalling principles like rapid logging and using key symbols (•, –, >).

Exercise Template

Track Your Action, Daily Reminder of Your Intention

Action plan trackers, also known as habit trackers, are powerful tools for honouring the process of achieving your goals. Imagine a simple grid with twelve columns representing months and thirty-one rows for each day. Fill it with symbols that represent the habits propelling you toward your goals.

Let's say you want to prioritize being healthier and translate your wish into the S.M.A.R.T. goal of 'exercise regularly twice or thrice a week'. Your tracker might include daily action represented by distinct symbols, for example, jogging (♥), going to the gym (♥), or attending yoga class (x). Drawing these symbols on each day you do these activities should become a daily ritual, a visual representation of your commitment to growth.

The magic of habit/action plan trackers extends beyond just recording actions. Over time, your tracker becomes a window into your progress. You can easily see:

- **Consistency:** Glance at the grid and instantly assess how consistently you've committed to progress towards your goals.
- **Progress:** Witness the accumulation of your efforts.

- **Effectiveness:** Analyse patterns and identify areas for improvement, allowing you to refine your approach as needed. For example, you notice that the grids tend to be empty a week before your period or after payday. It can help evaluate your behaviour and what you want to do about it.

Habit trackers aren't limited to a single goal. Think of them as modular building blocks. Within one journal, you can create multiple trackers—one for physical health and another for personal development (reading a self-improvement book, attending a webinarW, or listening to a podcast).

These visual reminders become a source of motivation. Seeing a row filled with symbols becomes a badge of honour, representing your self-discipline. Conversely, empty squares act as a reminder for you to get back on track.

Remember, habit trackers are not about striving for perfection. They're about progress. Don't be discouraged by missed days; pick yourself up and keep moving forward.

Habit / Action plan tracker

year : ________

goals :

____

____

____

Habit / action plan :

- ________
- ________
- ________

	1	2	3	4	5	6	7	8	9	10	11	12
1												
2												
3												
4												
5												
6												
7												
8												
9												
10												
11												
12												
13												
14												
15												
16												
17												
18												
19												
20												
21												
22												
23												
24												
25												
26												
27												
28												
29												
30												
31												
=												

example of How to Fill a

Habit / Action plan tracker

year: 2024

goals:

to exercise regularly, 2-3 times a week and be healthier

Habit / action plan:

- ● Jogging
- ♥ gym
- ⊗ Yoga

draw these symbols if you do it on the day

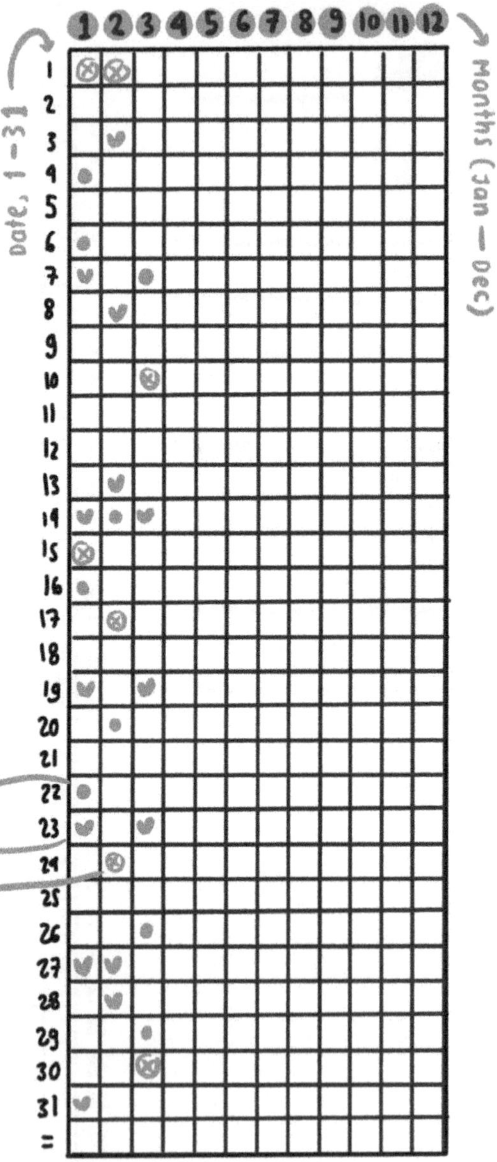

Exercise Template

Is It Near? Is It Far? Track with a Progress Bar

While habit/action plan trackers are fantastic for long-term goals, what about those specific, time-bound projects that demand more focus on progress? Try the progress bar template as a way to visualize our journey toward a well-defined objective.

A progress bar is more like a personalized roadmap. It targets a single goal with a set timeframe. Imagine you want to write a book and submit a manuscript to a publisher by the end of the year. Such a monumental task! Here's how a progress bar works:

- Create a simple grid with the Y-axis representing the time unit of your choice (days, months, etc.) and the X-axis representing progress. In the case of writing a book, you can measure progress by the number of pages written, chapters completed, or any unit that reflects your movement toward the finish line.
- Mark your progress on the grid each time unit (in this example, every month). Filling the bar may become a visual reward, demonstrating your progress.

This isn't just about filling the bar. As time progresses, the tracker becomes a valuable evaluation tool. You can assess your:

- **Discipline:** Analyse the consistency of your progress per time unit (daily, weekly, monthly).
- **Pace:** Identify if you need to adjust your workload division to meet your deadline.
- **Motivation:** Seeing the progress bar fill can be a powerful motivator, keeping you focused on your goal.

Progress bar trackers are versatile. Here are some additional application examples:

- **Savings tracker:** Track your monthly savings progress, visualizing how much closer you are to your financial goal.
- **Fitness tracker:** Chart your workout progress by recording the number of steps, kilometres run, or exercise duration.
- **Skill development:** Measure your progress in learning a new language, playing an instrument, or mastering any skill by using relevant metrics.

Since there's no one-size-fits-all approach, you can design your progress bar tracker in your journal, use a spreadsheet, or explore apps that offer similar functionalities.

The essence is to find a system that works for you by visualizing it. As the progress bar fills, celebrate your mini-wins and gain the confidence to keep going!

Self-Improved Me Note

Have fun with your progress bar. Use stickers or washi tape to mark your progress!

how to create a progress bar template:

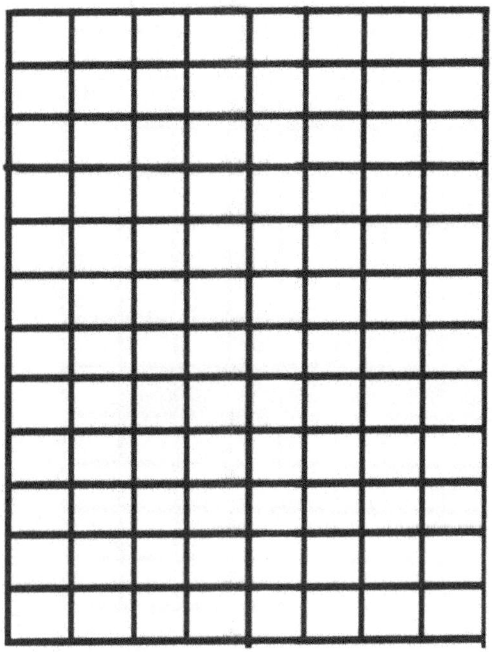

how to create a progress bar template:

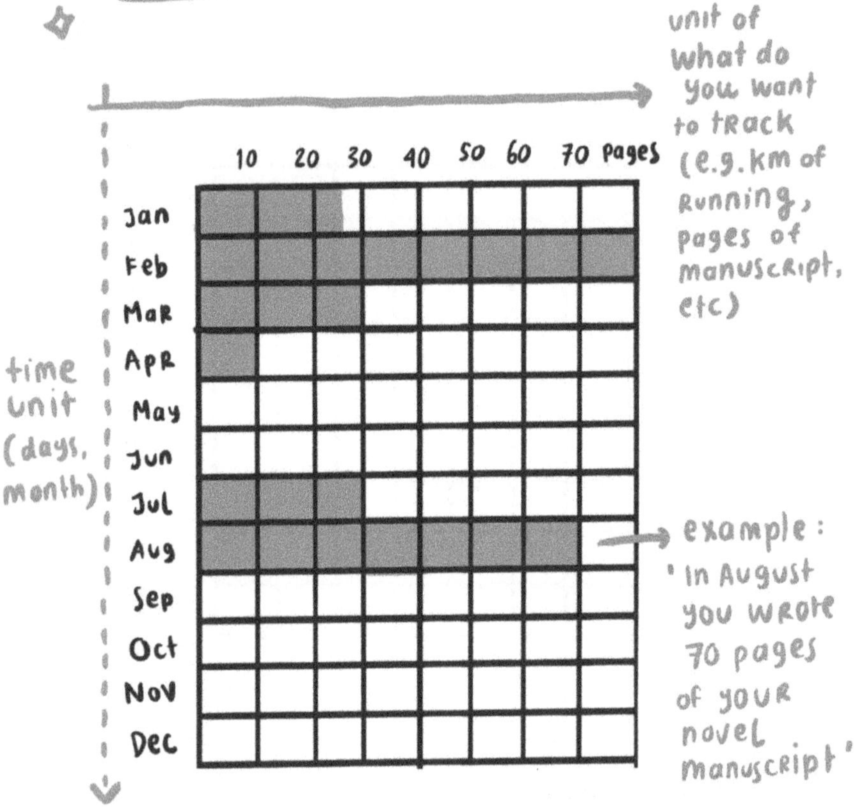

It Is Not Always About Doing, Getting, or Having More

With all the productivity tools and frameworks, we might perceive growing and making progress as doing, getting, or having more. Doing more projects, getting more money, having more knowledge, etc. Without realizing it, we may worry when life seems stagnant, let alone going backward. Then, we usually associate stagnation with matters of performance and strategy. For example, when our business profits don't grow, we may want to check our strategy. *Is it incorrect? Is the implementation inappropriate? How do I fix it?*

However, sometimes, we might need to step back and see the bigger picture. Maybe it's time that we revisit our intentions. *Why did I build this business in the first place? To be a billionaire in the future, or to do work that brings greater good to many people?*

Checking back on our intentions allows us to reframe the situation and make different decisions. Accepting stagnation could mean we've grown in a different direction. Even the tallest human stops growing taller at some point but gets more mature. The same goes for our personal progress and growth. Maybe our progress has manifested as stability. Perhaps, growth means a more peaceful afternoon and better sleep at night. Maybe, growing as a person for someone would mean having fewer friends but more meaningful relationships.

Using productivity tools like progress trackers is a very important step for better self-awareness, but self-improvement is also about seeing the bigger picture, and the ultimate process of self-discovery lies in reflection.

sometimes you feel that you're
NOT PROGRESSING ...

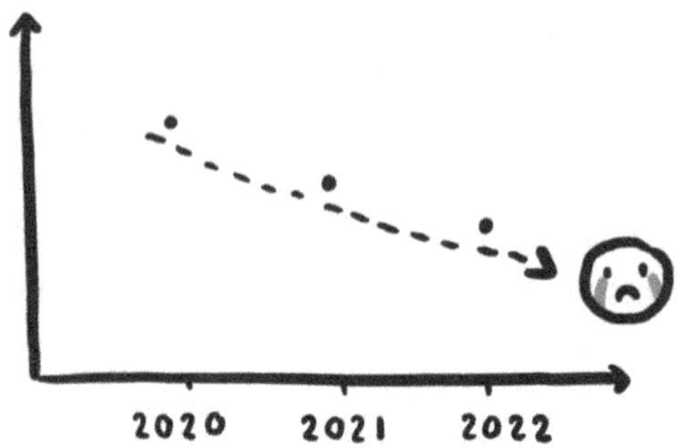

but life is a long game,
so you need to zoom out ...

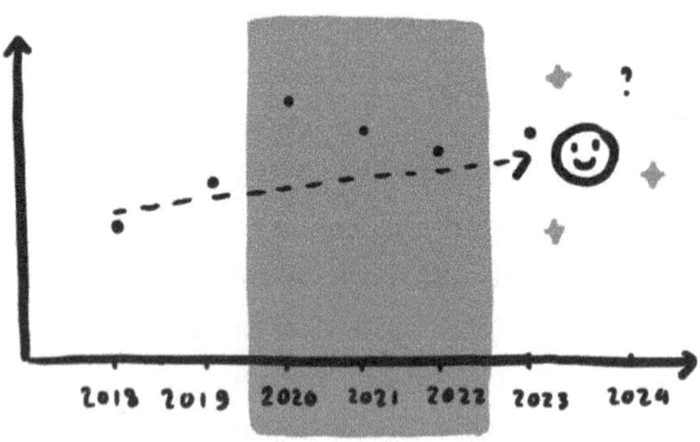

and get the big picture.

letting go is a
form of progress
too ...

grow from within:

self-reflection and EVALUATION

CHAPTER 8

GROW FROM WITHIN: SELF-REFLECTION AND EVALUATION

Self-Improvement, Self-Reflection, Self-Awareness, Repeat

To close the loop of the self-discovery cycle, after self-improvement comes self-reflection and evaluation. This isn't just about telling yourself what you failed or succeeded at; it's about gaining a deeper understanding of yourself and leveraging that knowledge for future growth.

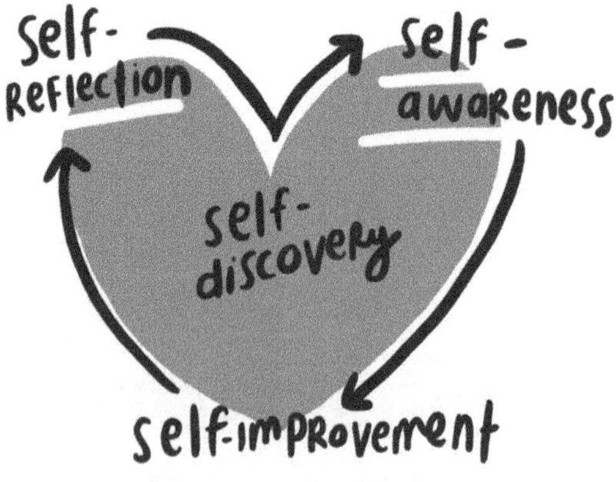

After self-reflection comes better self-awareness

how well do you know yourself?

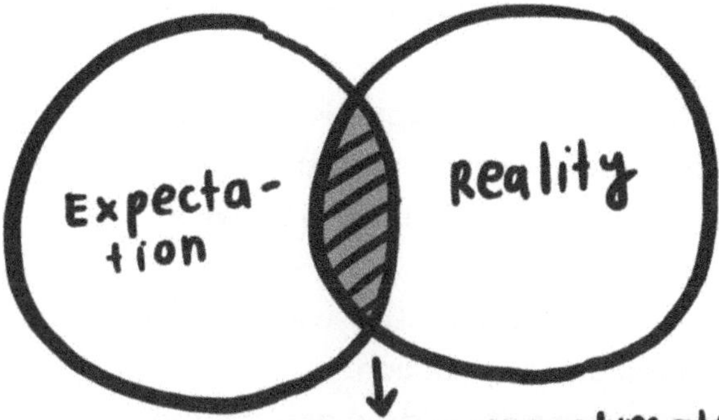

Sign that you often underestimate or overestimate yourself

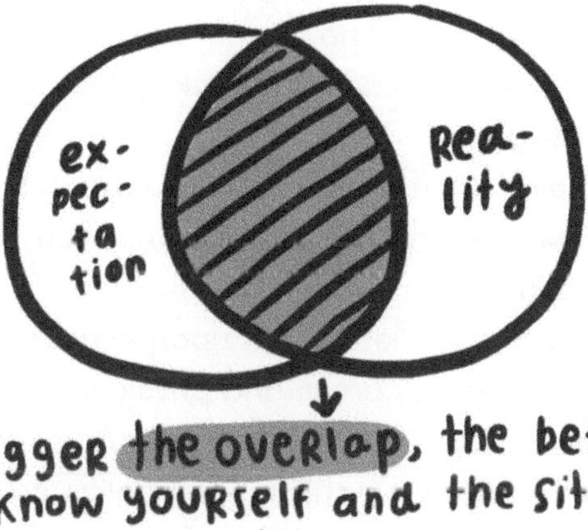

the bigger the overlap, the better you know yourself and the situations you're in ...

* Adapted from Peter F Drucker in Mikael Krogerus' *Decision Book* (2018)

As management guru Peter F. Drucker mentioned, combining self-awareness with your strengths is the key to achieving the best results. The thing is, we often misjudge ourselves. We set expectations that are either too high or too low, holding our progress up.

The illustration in this chapter is called feedback analysis, a tool to compare expectations with reality (Krogerus, 2018). Feedback analysis examines the gap between:

- **Plans vs execution:** Did we follow through on our intended course of action?
- **Targets vs results:** Did we achieve the goals we set for ourselves?

This self-evaluation is not only about measuring our capacity to 'do' things, but it also sheds light on our planning skills and execution abilities. This knowledge and awareness about ourselves help us in the process of making important decisions and setting new goals.

Imagine being offered a side hustle opportunity as a social media manager for your friend's start-up. You might initially feel interested and think you have the time (plus, it's a bit hard to say no to this friend). Yet, upon evaluating your goal map (prioritizing family, career, and physical health) and your tracked progress, which also shows your current commitments (making time to tutor your children, an online course for work certification, and going to the gym twice a week), you may realize you're already stretched thin. Self-reflection helps you make informed decisions that align with your capacity.

Beyond decision-making, this reflection helps you set new goals and targets. Should you maintain the existing goals? (Is the online course worth it? Should you delegate the tutoring?) Should you craft some new goals? (Can you still push a volunteering commitment there?) Self-reflection and evaluation provide valuable insights.

You may also notice some things about yourself that you weren't aware of before. You might discover that you're able to do more than you think when everything is scheduled properly. You may realize that some commitments really spark joy and boost your spirit to do the other things.

At the end of the day, self-reflection and evaluation is a continuous learning process that empowers us to reach our full potential.

Self-Improved Me Note

Without overthinking it, try to recreate the feedback analysis chart on this chapter based on your experience last year. How big is the overlap? How good are you at predicting yourself?

Exercise Template

Revisit Your Wheel of Life—Is Life a Little Less Bumpy Now?

Remember the Wheel of Life we filled in to set our goals? As a form of self-reflection, let's revisit it! Follow these steps:

- **Redraw your wheel:** Recreate your Wheel of Life, honestly reflecting on your current state in each area.
- **Compare and contrast:** Juxtapose your new wheel with the previous one. Notice the shifts – big or small. Has the overall shape improved? If you compare with your previous wheel, how would you feel about riding a vehicle with such a shape? Is life a little less bumpy now?

Self-Improved Me Note

Remember that the ideal Wheel of Life is a dynamic concept, not a static destination. The comparison should boost your motivation, not discourage you. It's a tool to identify areas for continued growth and celebrate your journey towards a more fulfilling life.

Check in on yourself again using the wheel of life

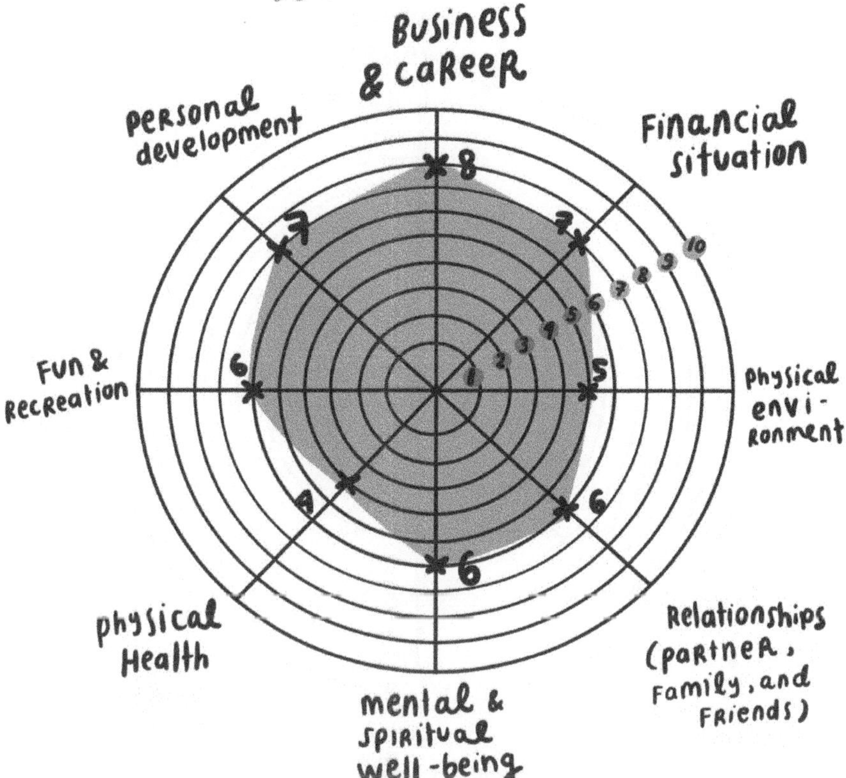

Compare your current wheel of life with the previous one. How do you feel about the change?

date: _/_/__

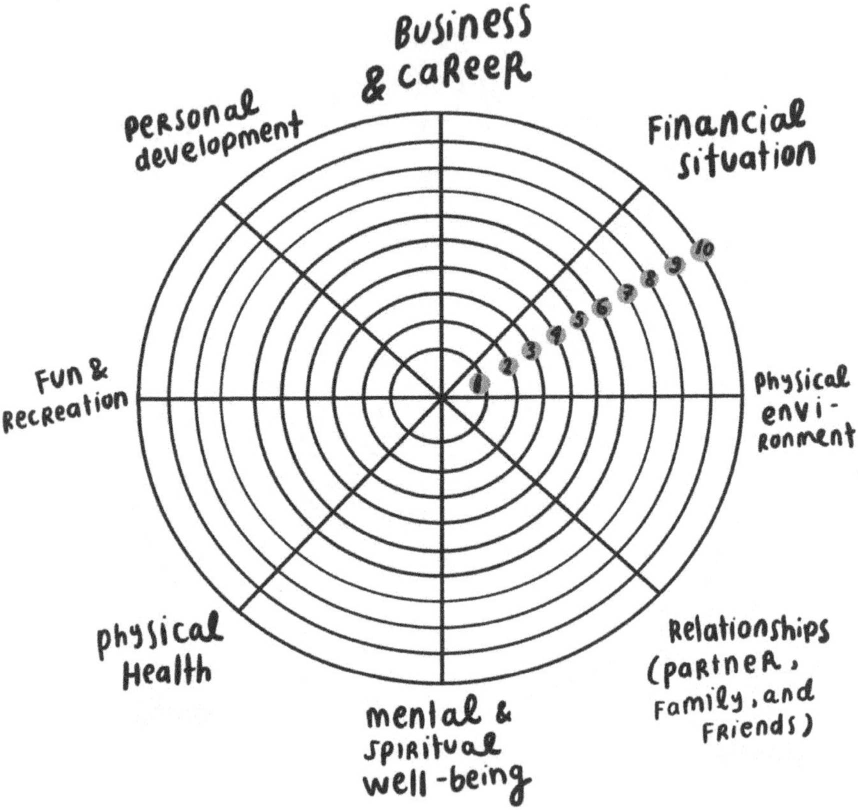

Business & career
Financial situation
Physical envi-ronment
Relationships (partner, family, and friends)
mental & spiritual well-being
physical Health
Fun & Recreation
personal development
1
2
3
4
5
6
7
8
9
10

Exercise Template

Did You Achieve that Plan? Did You Plan What You Achieve?

Writing down our self-evaluation in a matrix with two axes—'achieved vs not achieved' and 'planned vs unplanned'—can be a powerful tool for analysing our plans and their outcomes. This framework helps us identify areas for improvement and celebrate unexpected achievements.

- **Evaluating missed goals:** When a goal is planned but not achieved, there are two key questions. Was the goal itself flawed, or was it the execution problem? You may check if the goal was indeed unattainable or just poorly defined. The execution process, on the other hand, relates to our capacity and ability to achieve the goal. Here, factors like consistency, resource allocation, and focus can come into play. Additionally, unforeseen circumstances beyond our control can also derail our plans. An injury might force us to stop jogging, or a global economic crisis might lead to mass layoffs, disrupting our career paths.
- **Embracing unplanned achievements:** Self-evaluation isn't just about missed targets; it should also celebrate the unplanned wins. Remember the surge of creativity during the COVID-19 pandemic? Many people embraced new experiences—taking online courses for the first time or pivoting their businesses in unique directions. These unplanned achievements deserve a place in our self-evaluation. In this case, we can consider including them as new goals in the future.

- **Evaluating achieved goals:** What about when things go as planned, and our target is achieved? Do we need to assess? Yes. It doesn't mean that there is nothing else we can improve. Consider modifying the target to increase the challenge or even dropping it altogether. For example, you planned to learn Japanese, and the goal was to get certified in JLPT N5 (the first and easiest level). After you achieve it, you can evaluate whether you want to continue and pursue the N4 level or drop it and learn another language instead.

Try to use this matrix and get ready to set better goals!

questions for evaluation

	Achieved	NOT achieved
Planned	♥ Is this goal challenging enough? Is it too easy? ♥ Should I do it again next time? ♥ Should I modify the target?	♥ Is this goal achievable? Is it too hard? ♥ If it is achievable, what was the problem? ↳ was it something I could control? ♥ Is it worth it to try again next time?
Unplanned	♥ How was it achieved? Was it something I could control? or totally unpredictable? ♥ Should it be put on the goals list next time?	* space for fresh ideas *

goals evaluation exercise

	Achieved	NOT achieved
Planned		
Unplanned		

Honesty Is the Best Policy, but Even from You to You, It Is Never Easy

Journalling in the form of written self-reflection sounds simple. We might think of it as just a little conversation with ourselves. However, as Timothy Wilson, an American psychologist, suggests, we might be surprised by the truth: 'We are strangers to ourselves.' We often hold onto illusions of self-awareness, believing we understand our motivations better than anyone.

Rory Sutherland, a behavioural science expert, echoes this sentiment in his book *Alchemy*. He reminds us: 'People don't think what they feel, they don't say what they think, and they don't do what they say.' In other words, denial is a powerful force that often happens subconsciously.

For example, some of us, mothers, get so ambitious when it comes to scheduling our children's endless extracurricular activities. We might say that we do that for our children so they can have a bright future, but if we dig deeper, we may find other reasons. Perhaps, through honest self-reflection, we discover those unspoken insecurities—the fear that our children will miss out and get left behind.

This is where writing becomes a powerful tool for self-discovery. *Writing self-reflection is more than just conveying ideas—it's a way of crystallizing them. As we put pen to paper, the gaps in our logic and inconsistencies in our beliefs come to light.* The writing process exposes our assumptions, forcing us to consider alternative perspectives.

Frequent writing isn't only useful to sharpen our communication skills; it helps the process of self-discovery. Pouring down our feelings into a journal is like a process of peeling back the layers of denial and confronting

It takes courage and practice to be honest with yourself.

those uncomfortable truths hidden beneath. *That's why it takes courage and practice to be honest with ourselves.* It forces us to deal with complex emotions, hidden fears, and sometimes primal motivations.

Be brave. Write it down.

Self-Improved Me Note

A blank page sometimes becomes a hurdle for journalling for self-reflection. Guided journals with prompts can help you start writing and may lead to deeper reflection. Find journalling prompts that suit your needs. Search engines and AI assistance are your best friends!

Journalling prompts!
What was one thing I did well this week?
what was one thing I struggled with?
Did I make any decisions that went against my core values?
How can I be more mindful about my values in the future?
Am I on track to achieve my goals?
what steps did I take this week to move closer to them?
on a scale 1-10, how moti-vated am I feeling about my goals?
1 2 3 4 5 6 7 8 9 10
You can also explore more prompts with AI!

Thanks for Your Feedback, (Maybe) I'll Get Back

Besides self-reflection and evaluation, others' feedback may also give important insights into our journey. Taking them into account includes information from perspectives that are blind spots for us. Nevertheless, not all feedback is worth processing.

Let's imagine you just started an accessories business online, and for marketing purposes, you create short video content on Instagram. When someone comments, 'What, your hands are ugly and wrinkled,' you should instantly ignore it because it's irrelevant. Then another person comments, 'Duh, this is such a cute item, but why is it so expensive???' Should this feedback be processed? It depends on whether the person represents your target market. If yes, their feedback might improve the probability of achieving your objective. You can use this feedback to re-evaluate your pricing strategy or emphasize the unique value proposition that justifies the cost.

If not, the input should be considered with less urgency as we are targeting a different market. After all, in life, we can't serve and please everyone with our limited resources.

The key lies in clarity. Having a clear understanding of your work; your own values and objectives empower you to discern which feedback is truly valuable and which is best left ignored.

After all, keep creating. Analyse the relevant feedback, follow up with improvements, and keep going!

How should I process
Feedback ?

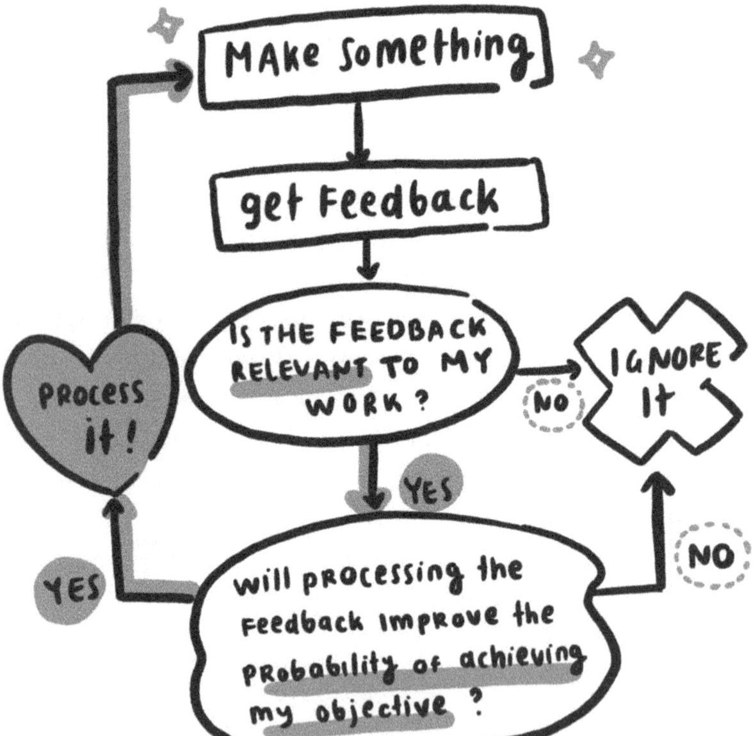
Make something
get Feedback
IS THE FEEDBACK RELEVANT TO MY WORK ?
NO
IGNORE It
YES
will processing the Feedback improve the probability of achieving my objective ?
NO
YES
PROCESS it!

turn
Reflection
into
Better
Intention

CHAPTER 9

TURN REFLECTION INTO BETTER INTENTION

New Year, Now Me

We are sometimes too obsessed with the 'New Year, New Me' tagline. The pressure to completely reinvent ourselves drives us to write something fancy on the list and overpromise ourselves. It ignites the need to level up the goals and targets. However, maintaining existing resolutions is a victory in itself, and stability as a form of achievement is often undervalued. Sometimes, the most significant progress happens within a framework of stability. Remember, consistency is key! Sticking to the healthy eating plan you established last year is a major achievement, not a sign of stagnation.

Moreover, after self-reflection and evaluation, you are allowed to level down some targets or eliminate some goals. It might be a sign that you gained more clarity and that you know yourself better. In fact, it's easy to make things more complicated and cluttered. But to make life simple requires us to let go. As artist Georgia O'Keefe said, 'It is only by selection, by elimination and by emphasis that we get at the real meaning of things.'

New Year ~~New~~ Me

updated version

So, celebrate your achievements!
Celebrate your consistency and stability!
Celebrate having less to know yourself even more.
After all, growth is a journey, not a destination.

Take a Detour, Letting Go of Your Dreams

For a goal-oriented person, unlearning a long-held dream can take a lot of work. Emotional attachment is inevitable after a certain period of planning, making tremendous efforts, and meticulous progress tracking. In behavioural science, it is called the 'sunk cost fallacy', where we cling to something because we've heavily invested in it, even if circumstances change.

In his book *Think Again: The Power of Knowing What You Don't Know,* Adam Grant mentions that in the unlearning process, grit can be an inhibitor of rethinking. Grit is the combination of passion and perseverance, and research shows that it can play an essential role in motivating someone to accomplish long-term goals. However, gritty people are more willing to stay the course in tasks at which they're failing, even when success is impossible.

Imagine that you've always believed you want to be a career woman and set the SMART goal to reach a C-level position in fifteen years. After seven years of working, you've reached a manager position and are now married with two kids. You start to feel overwhelmed by the task juggling, and you feel like you want to resign from your job because you think that your kids need you, and you need to take care of your mental health.

I'm gonna be a career woman! I'll be in a C-Level position!
IN MY 20s
I just want my kids to be healthy and my family to be happy
IN MY 30s
now my kids are older, it's time for me to learn something new again...
maybe, in my 40s...

This is not an easy decision to make because you've spent years investing your time and effort in your career. It has also somewhat become your identity—you are *that* career woman. As your identity is now tied to your goal, it's even harder to unlearn and start something anew. You might also feel the fear of failure or of being a quitter.

Some tips to navigate this situation:

- **Revisit your 'why':** Ask yourself again about why you want to reach that goal. Is it really the position that you're looking for? Could it be that what you want is earning good income or you're passionate about being a leader? What is it that you really want?
- **Explore alternative paths:** Consider whether you can reach that goal through other means. Do you think good income can also come from having a side business or stock trading from home? Do you think your leadership can be useful in the nonprofit community around you? Is there a way to reach your goal?
- **Embrace the pivot:** Be open to the possibility that the next step might be pivoting. Pivoting is not quitting. Pivoting is changing direction. It's about adjusting your course while still aiming for a similar objective. It's a strategic shift in approach due to new information, obstacles, or opportunities. Pivoting is driven by a desire to improve or adapt. It's a proactive response to find a more effective way to achieve your goals.

Growth often happens in unexpected territories. You may have outgrown your dreams and think you're stuck because you don't think you can step back and take a detour. However, the path you're yet to discover may lead to a future that's even more fulfilling than the one you had originally envisioned.

Restart Small, Restart Courageously

Self-reflection and evaluation can be nice and motivation-boosting when you're doing well. However, it can be nightmare for us who are feeling like everything is falling apart. When you're juggling, dropping one ball might lead to dropping all of them. Suddenly, everything that was once in your hands, is now on the floor, falling and ruining the show. Picking up all the pieces can be hard and emotionally draining. Writing mistakes down and admitting that you didn't make progress and messed up is undoubtedly dreadful.

For example, when our business fails, it will affect our financial situation and probably our mental well-being. It will disturb our sleep and physical health. Then, this might lead to a more strained relationship with our spouse and children. One thing leads to another, so quickly taking action to mitigate one or two problems might save us from further damage. It requires us to be courageous.

Failure can be paralysing, but after some time, we need to bounce back. Take the small steps at first to rebuild our confidence. Pick up the easiest ball to reach and slowly get the others back. Go for a walk and work for your physical health, it might clear your mind, lighten up your mood, and make it easier for you to sleep better. This might get you communicating better to you closest ones and receiving support might ease up your pain a bit and nudge you to start something else.

Restart your journey. Try to draw your Wheel of Life again and accept whatever shape it is. After a break, be brave to assess your failure and learn from it. It's not easy but self-reflection is a there are times when we feel like everything is falling apart. when life feels too much to handle.

but that's okay.
we can pick the pieces up one by one. bit by bit.

step towards recovery. Remember to recheck your core values, revisit your intention, and redefine your success.

Find your reason to restart courageously.

Do it at your own pace but do it.

Start Small, Start Now

'So now, should I start journalling? Should I try drawing my Wheel of Life?'

After reading this book, you might feel encouraged to do something out of character. You might want to grab some papers and a ruler to follow the exercises. Or else, you might ask yourself, 'Will it work? What if I fail? What if it is not for me?'

This kind of hesitation may hold you back from taking action but here's a truth: *Nobody actually cares about your failure as much as you think they do.*

This book offers a sort of toolkit, not a script. It doesn't prescribe a one-size-fits-all method but instead emphasizes the importance of the process of self-discovery. Maybe journalling resonates with you, but perhaps a different approach sparks your creativity better. Don't be afraid to experiment and fail. Maybe you'll find yourself abandoning your habit tracker and later you forget about the goals evaluation table all together. Still, it's an action that will spark some valuable insight about yourself.

So take action! Give it a try. The biggest hurdle is often simply starting. Shush your inner critic, grab that pen, and draw that (imperfect) Wheel of Life. Download that habit tracker, even if it's just for a week. Start small, be flexible, and have fun with the process!

CUT HERE TO CLAIM a little REWARD FOR YOURSELF

Summary in a Chart

Self-Improved ME, Self-Discovery!

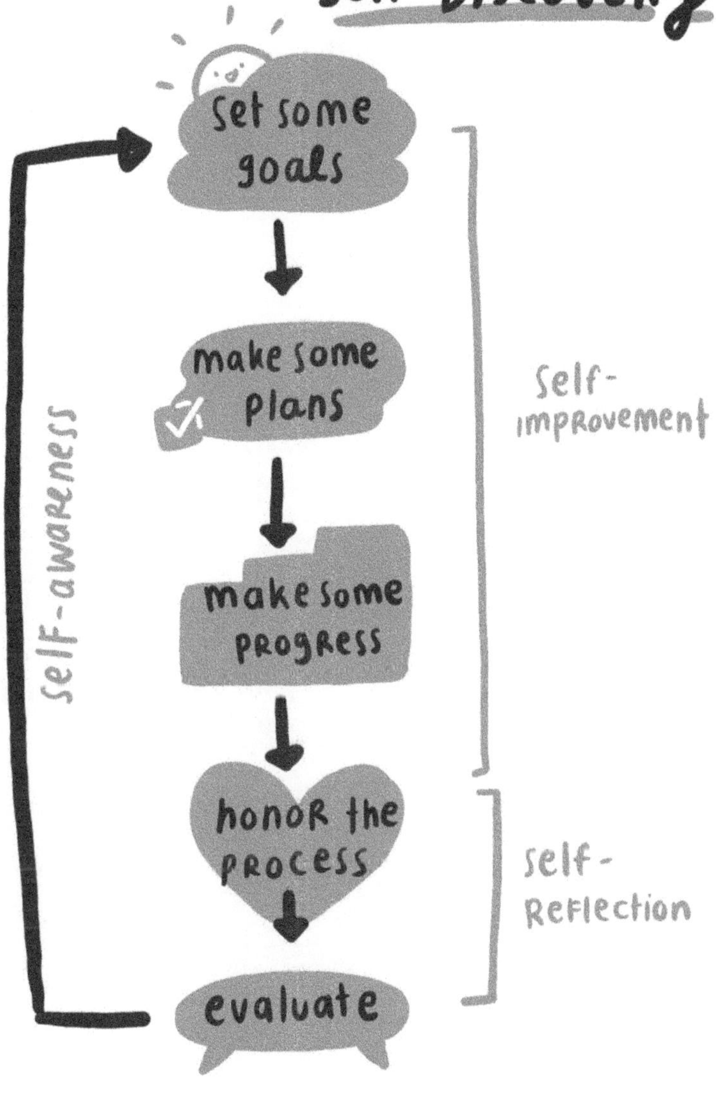

REFERENCES

Ansari, Aziz, et al. *Modern Romance*. Hauteville, 2017.

Byrne, Una. "Wheel of Life." *Business Information Review*, vol. 22, no. 2, 2005, pp. 123–130, doi:10.1177/0266382105054770

Clear, James. *Atomic Habits: An Easy & Proven Way to Build Good Habits & Break Bad Ones*. Avery, An Imprint of Penguin Random House, 2018.

Darley, John M., and C. Daniel Batson. "'From Jerusalem to Jericho': A Study of Situational and Dispositional Variables in Helping Behavior." *Journal of Personality and Social Psychology*, vol. 27, no. 1, July 1973, pp. 100–108, doi:10.1037/h0034449.

Duhigg, Charles. *The Power of Habit*. Random House, 2014.

Dweck, Carol S. *Mindset: Changing the Way You Think to Fulfil Your Potential*. Robinson, 2017.

Gilbert, Daniel Todd. *Stumbling on Happiness*. Vintage Books, A Division of Random House, 2007.

Grant, Adam M. *Think Again: The Power of Knowing What You Don't Know*. Viking, 2021.

Hirsch, Patricia, Iring Koch, and Julia Karbach. "Putting a Stereotype to the Test: The Case of Gender Differences in Multitasking Costs in Task-Switching and Dual-Task Situations." *PLOS ONE*, vol. 14, no. 8, 14 Aug. 2019, doi:10.1371/journal.pone.0220150.

Holiday, Ryan. *Discipline Is Destiny: The Power of Self-Control.* Portfolio, 2022.

Szameitat, André J., Yasmin Hamaida, Rebecca S. Tulley, Rahmi Saylik, and Pauldy C. J. Otermans. "'Women Are Better than Men'–Public Beliefs on Gender Differences and Other Aspects in Multitasking." *PLOS ONE*, vol. 10, no. 10, 19 Oct. 2015, doi:10.1371/journal.pone.0140371.

Krogerus, Mikael. *Decision Book: Fifty Models for Strategic Thinking*. W. W. Norton & Company, 2018.

Lewrick, Michael, Jean-Paul Thommen and Larry Leifer. *The Design Thinking Life Playbook: Empower Yourself, Embrace Change, and Visualize a Joyful Life*. John Wiley & Sons, 2020.

Pang, Alex Soojung-Kim. *Rest: Why You Get More Done When You Work Less*. Perseus Books, 2016.

Pietsch, Bryan. "Elon Musk Says Every Company Should Maximize the 'curve of Customer Happiness' - Here's What That Means." *Business Insider*, 30 Apr. 2020, www.businessinsider.com/elon-musk-advice-to-companies-maximize-curve-of-customer-happiness-2020-4. Accessed 6 May 2024.

Stein, Randy, and Alexander B. Swan. "Evaluating the Validity of Myers-Briggs Type Indicator Theory: A Teaching Tool and Window into Intuitive Psychology." *Social and Personality Psychology Compass*, vol. 13, no. 2, 25 Jan. 2019, doi:10.1111/spc3.12434.

Stone, Douglas, Bruce Patton, and Sheila Heen. *Difficult Conversations: How to Discuss What Matters Most*. Penguin Books, 2023.

Sutherland, Rory. *Alchemy: The Dark Art and Curious Science of Creating Magic in Brands, Business, and Life*. Mariner Books, 2019.

Storr, Will. *The Status Game*. William Collins, 2022.

Thiagarajan, Maya. *Beyond the Tiger Mom: East-West Parenting for the Global Age*. Tuttle Publishing, 2018.

Tversky, Amos, and Daniel Kahneman. “Judgment under Uncertainty: Heuristics and Biases.” *Science*, vol. 185, no. 4157, 27 Sept. 1974, pp. 1124–1131, doi:10.1126/science.185.4157.1124.

Zook, Jason. “The Theory of the 3 Whys | Inc.Com.” *Inc.*, 8 Jan. 2018, www.inc.com/jason-surfrapp/the-theory-of-the-3-whys.html. Accessed 6 May 2024.

ACKNOWLEDGMENTS

This book wouldn't have been possible without the love and support of those who believed in me.

First and foremost, I want to express my deepest gratitude to my family. To my super-supportive husband, Anggun, and my beloved children, Isa and Nala, thank you for being awesome cheerleaders. To my parents, Ayah and Bunda, my brother, Zakki, and my in-laws, your encouragement and unwavering support mean the world to me. Special shout out to my assistants at home to whom I delegate the laundry, cooking, and . . . well, many other things.

I'm also incredibly grateful to the Penguin Random House SEA team. Nora Nazarene, thank you for taking a chance on me and believing in this project. To my editors, Divya, Swadha, and Sneha, your meticulous work and patience are truly appreciated. Thank you so much for bearing with my handwriting (and all the typos, OMG!) To Adviata from the design team for her massive help with placing the illustrations (what a manuscript, right?), thank you!

Special shout out to Garima, who opened the door in the first place, I hope we cross paths again! To Ira, my Indonesian editor and the Gramedia International Team, thank you!

And last but certainly not least, I want to thank my incredible community. To the BBBBabes of the BBB Book Club, Meita, Fitri, Amel, Adin, and all the volunteers and members, your enthusiasm and support have been a constant source of inspiration. To my wonderful friends, Nadya, Shanti, the ISFiT gang, Fungs (Sari, I do cherish our reel-ationship), and everyone who has sent me kind words and (requests for) memes, your friendship and support mean more than you know!